First published in 1982 by
**Jupiter Cantab Ltd.**
This 35th Anniversary Edition
published in 2017 by
**Andrews UK Limited**
www.andrewsuk.com

© Copyright 1982, 2017 Andrews UK Limited

Jupiter Ace Trademark and brand owned by
Andrews UK Limited from 2015

# 35 Years On, The Jupiter Ace Lives Again!

Launched at the peak of the legendary 1980's microcomputer rivalry, the Jupiter ACE was created by the vexed designers of the Sinclair Spectrum and became the most intriguing machine of them all.

> "Clive Sinclair was making all this money out of us, why shouldn't we just make our own computer and make the money for ourselves"
> *-Steve Vickers*

And with its unconventional FORTH system...

> "It's ten times faster than BASIC"
> *-Richard Altwasser*

The ACE was a significant machine running inspired software, but it struggled to compete in a marketplace increasingly dominated by home users wanting to play games with colour and sound. The monochrome display, tiny beeper and unfamiliar language all combined to limit its popular appeal, and very soon the ACE was in financial trouble. Jupiter Cantab Ltd, the short-lived company set up by Vickers and Altwasser to produce the machine, ceased trading during the autumn of 1983 and was in liquidation by November.

But the ACE had a second chance...

At a meeting on 6th February 1984 with Dennis Cross, the appointed Liquidator of Jupiter Cantab, it was agreed that Boldfield Computing would make a staged purchase of all the assets and stock, starting two weeks later on 21st February. Mail order sales commenced straightaway, with Boldfield Computing working quickly to add the missing software and accessories that would make the ACE viable as a machine for enthusiasts. A full brochure of products was launched during the summer of '84, and a dedicated Jupiter ACE showroom opened in Cambridge later the same year.

With the ACE now successfully selling to a niche market, and having bought up all the known stockpiles in Britain, Boldfield scoured the European outlets too, bringing back more ACEs and converting them to the UK standard. Boldfield Computing's commitment and support for the product was maintained well into 1986 – allowing the Jupiter ACE to outlast its rivals with dignity, and be assured its place in history.

The original Boldfield directors retained the Jupiter ACE brand, along with a treasure trove of its historic artefacts', but in 2015 they decided the time had come to pass on this iconic brand to another custodian. The new owners, Andrews UK Limited, are working with others not only to preserve the past, but also secure the future of the much-loved Jupiter ACE.

www.jupiter-ace.com

www.jupiterace.uk

# Contents

Contents

# Introduction

In 1950 the National Physical Laboratory made the Pilot ACE (Automatic Computing Engine), one of the earliest British computers. Internally it could store an amount of information measured as 1¼ Kilobytes, it took 32 microseconds to perform its simplest operation and, with its large number of wires, valves and tubes filled with mercury, occupied a space the size of a small kitchen. Most of its remains can now be seen in the Science Museum at South Kensington.

Based on the Pilot ACE, English Electric developed their DEUCE (Digital Electronic Universal Computing Engine). Over six years they sold about forty of these, costing between £30,000 and £40,000 each.

Now, in 1982, Jupiter Cantab Ltd have produced their own Ace. It can store 3 Kilobytes of information (which can easily be extended) and has an extra 8 Kilobytes of program built into it permanently; the Z80A microprocessor at its heart executes its simplest instruction in just over 1 microsecond, and it is small enough to rest in your lap. Thousands of them will be made, costing less than £100 each.

How do we at Jupiter Cantab manage it? Not by being extraordinarily clever (although, of course, we are). We are simply the beneficiaries of thirty-two years of development that invented the printed circuit board, the transistor, and then methods of packing thousands of transistors onto one small silicon chip; and in the process transformed computers into machines for everyone.

# Chapter 1

## SETTING UP THE ACE

This manual is delivered with a few accessories, which you should check:

1. A Jupiter Ace computer.

2. A mains adaptor, which converts mains electricity into a low voltage suitable for the Ace. It will work properly only in certain countries (normally including the one to which the Ace was delivered), so if you take your Ace abroad you may need a different mains adaptor.
  The mains adaptor is a heavy plastic box, three or four inches in size, and extending from it is a lead with a jack plug at the end.

3. A video lead. This is a single coaxial lead with a phono plug at one end and an aerial plug at the other. It is used to connect the Ace to a television.

4. A pair of leads with jack plugs at both ends, used to connect the Ace to a cassette tape recorder. The plugs are colour-coded, so that you can tell the two leads apart.

You will need to provide for yourself a mains electricity supply and a television, which must work on a 625 line 50Hz UHF system. (This is how most televisions in Britain work, but there are some older ones that don't. If your television can receive BBC2 then it should work with the Ace.)
  Later you will need a cassette tape recorder and tape, but these aren't immediately necessary.
  Having collected all these, plug the mains adaptor into the mains and switch on there, and plug its jack plug into the socket on the left-hand side of the Ace marked (underneath) 'POWER'. There is no switch on the Ace, so as soon as you do this it starts working. However, you won't know what it's doing until you connect it to the television, so that's the next step.
  Somewhere at the back of the television there should be a socket where the aerial plugs in; but instead of the usual aerial, you must plug in the video lead from the computer. Only one end will fit properly; the other end plugs in to the socket on the right-hand side of the Ace marked 'TV'
  Now plug the television into the mains (unless it uses batteries, of course), switch it on, turn its volume right down, and tune it to channel 36 UHF. (If it uses buttons to select the different channels, you'll have to pick one of these and find a way of tuning it in to the computer.)
  When you've tuned it just right the screen will be a uniform dark grey, except for a small white square near the bottom left-hand corner.

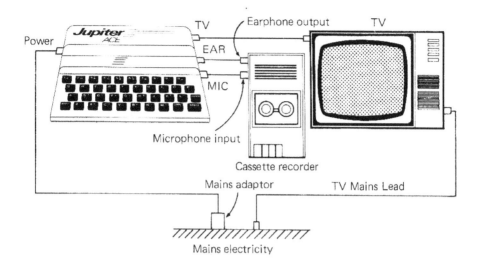

Mains electricity

(Now you've set it up, you can start pressing a few keys at random on the Ace keyboard, just to see what happens. You can always get back to the starting position by momentarily disconnecting the power supply from the Ace.)

The Ace understands a powerful computing language called FORTH. FORTH was invented around 1970 by Charles Moore, and was chosen for the Ace because of its speed, its economical use of computer memory, and the way a few simple concepts give an elegant power to the whole language.

If you already know about FORTH then you will use this manual largely for reference. Chapter 2 describes the input buffer, and Appendix D describes the principle features unique to Ace FORTH.

If you know nothing about FORTH but you want to learn how to use it, then this manual is for you. Start at the beginning and work right the way through. The exercises at the end of each chapter often make interesting points that the main part of the chapter doesn't cover, so don't overlook them even if you don't feel like doing them.

There remains a third group of Ace owners who aren't interested at all in programming it, but who have bought other people's programs on cassette tape and want to be able to run them. If you're in this third group, Chapters 2 and 3 should be enough to get you going.

# Chapter 2

## TYPING AT THE KEYBOARD

If you've never used a computer before, you're probably feeling a bit overawed, wondering what it's going to do. The answer is nothing, until you tell it by typing in your instructions at the keyboard. Try some random typing just to see what happens. If you get in a mess, remember that you can always clear the computer out by momentarily disconnecting it from its power supply.

The first thing you'll notice is that the characters (i.e. letters, digits, punctuation marks, symbols or anything else) you type appear at the bottom of the television screen. This area is called the *input buffer* and is where the computer will look for your instructions. If you type in enough to fill up a whole line (this is easily done by holding a key down for a few seconds, because it starts repeating itself), the line will move up to make some extra space beneath it: thus the input buffer has the power of expanding upwards if necessary.

Letters usually come up as lower case (small) letters, but, as on an ordinary typewriter, you can get capitals by using the SHIFT key (bottom left-hand corner). If you have this held down when you press a letter key, the letter will come out as a capital (try it).

There is another shift key called SYMBOL SHIFT (near the bottom right-hand corner, next to SPACE) that is used for typing in the symbols — full stop, comma, +, —, brackets and so on — that you can see in the corners of many of the keys. This works in the same way as the other, capitals, shift; you keep it held down while you press another key. For instance, to get '+' you hold down SYMBOL SHIFT, press the K key, and then let up both the keys.

---

Beware! Computers are very fussy that you should distinguish between the digit nought and the letter O. To make it absolutely clear, nought appears on the keyboard and television as 0, with a slash through it. It will be printed like that in the manual too.

You also need to distinguish between the digit one (1), the capital letter I, and the small letter L (l). On an ordinary typewriter you'd quite probably type a capital letter O for a nought and a small L for a one, but you mustn't do this with a computer. All ten digits are on the top row of the keyboard.

---

You may well be wondering by this stage why the computer isn't taking any notice of all this rubbish you've typed in. The reason is not that it's already noticed it's rubbish, but simply that it hasn't looked yet. It won't take any notice until you press what is just about the most important key on the keyboard, the one marked ENTER (on the right-hand side, one row up). Just pressing this means, 'OK computer, I've typed in your orders. Now go and obey them.'

If you press ENTER now, the most likely effect is that a . [?] will appear at the beginning. [?] means, 'Do you want to change any of this?', which in your case is a tactful way of telling you it doesn't understand a word you're saying. Clear the computer out by momentarily disconnecting the power, to give yourself a chance to type in orders that it does understand.

If you now press ENTER, the computer will print 'OK' on the television screen near the top — it has happily obeyed everything you typed in (i.e. nothing) and come back for more.

The first thing to remember is that, like us, the computer understands words-- not English words, however, but FORTH words. To make the distinction, we shall print FORTH words in **BOLD** type — not because you need somehow to type them into the computer in **BOLD**, but just so that you know whether we're using a word in a FORTH sense or an English sense.

Here's a FORTH word:

### VLIST

It stands for 'vocabulary list'. If, with the computer clear, you type in **VLIST** (it doesn't matter whether you use lower case letters or capitals or a mixture) and then press ENTER, you will see this (written in white on black):

### VLIST

```
     FORTH  UFLOAT  INT  FNEGATE  F/  F*  F
+  F—  LOAD  BVERIFY  VERIFY  BLOAD  B
SAVE  SAVE  LIST  EDIT  FORGET  REDEF
INE  EXIT  .  '  (  [  +LOOP  LOOP  DO  UN
TIL  REPEAT  BEGIN  THEN  ELSE  WHILE
 IF  ]  LEAVE  J  I'  I  DEFINITIONS  V
OCABULARY  IMMEDIATE  RUNS>  DOES>
COMPILER  CALL  DEFINER  ASCII  LITE
RAL  CONSTANT  VARIABLE  ALLOT  C,  ,
 CREATE  :  DECIMAL  MIN  MAX  XOR  AN
D  OR  2—  1—  2+  1+  D+  —  +  DNEGATE
NEGATE  U/MOD  */  *  MOD  /  */MOD  /M
OD  U*  D<  U<  <  >  =  0>  0<  0=  ABS  O
UT  IN  INKEY  BEEP  PLOT  AT  F.  EMIT
 CR  SPACES  SPACE  HOLD  CLS  #  #S  U
.  .  SIGN  #>  <#  TYPE  ROLL  PICK  OV
ER  ROT  ?DUP  R>  >R  !  @  C!  C@  SWAP
 DROP  DUP  SLOW  FAST  INVIS  VIS  CO
NVERT  NUMBER  EXECUTE  FIND  VLIST
WORD  RETYPE  QUERY  LINE  PAD  BAS
E  CURRENT  CONTEXT  HERE  ABORT  QUI
T OK
     ■
```

9

This is a complete list of all the words that the Ace understands when you first turn it on (its *dictionary*). *You* can see that some of them are the same as English words, some are abbreviations, some are mathematical, and some are strange combinations of symbols. Near the bottom you can see **VLIST** itself. (The **VLIST** at the top is just what you typed in, copied up as a record of your typing.) The 'OK' right at the end is not a FORTH word, but just what the computer says when it's finished your orders.

You can type in more than one word at once, like

## VLIST  VLIST

(The computer copies up the first **VLIST**, executes by it listing the dictionary, does the same with the second **VLIST,** and then prints OK.)

It is important to put spaces in between the words. If I suddenly flip and start running allmywordstogether or spli ttingt he mup then you still know what I'm trying to say, but the computer isn't so clever. It relies very much on having spaces in between words, and no spaces in the middle of a single word. On the other hand, a word can spill over from one line to the next, like

### VLI

### ST

with twenty eight spaces before the V, because the computer is hardly even aware of the separate lines within the input buffer.

To summarise,

● Typing from the keyboard goes to the *input buffer* at the bottom of the screen.

● Letters are usually in lower case, but you can get capitals by keeping the key marked SHIFT held down while you press the letter key.

● In the same way, you get punctuation marks and other symbols by using the SYMBOL SHIFT key.

● The computer has a built-in dictionary of 142 FORTH words that it understands, and you can type them in using lower case or capitals, as you wish.

● If you type more than one word into the input buffer, they must be separated by spaces.

● The computer doesn't start looking at what you've typed until you press ENTER. Then it takes the words from the input buffer one by one, copying each one up to the top for the record and then executing it.

● **VLIST** is a FORTH word. It tells the computer to write a list on the television of all the FORTH words in the dictionary.

● If the computer finds a word that it doesn't understand in the input buffer, it puts in a .**?** at the beginning.**?** means, 'Do you want to change any of this?'

*What if you make a typing mistake?*

So far the only cure you know is to disconnect the power supply, but there are much cleverer ways which rely on the cursor - the little white square that moves along as you type. This shows where the next character that you type will appear, so if you could somehow move it back to the middle of the line you could get characters to appear in the middle.

You do this using the cursor control keys, the ones marked ⇦, ⇧, ⇩ and ⇨ Although these are normally just the keys for 5, 6, 7 and 8, if you shift one - just as you would for capital letters, by holding SHIFT down - it will move the cursor in the direction of the arrow. Thus ⇦ is shifted 5, is shifted 6 and so on. (There is another up arrow, the ↑ that is symbols shifted H. This is not the same as ⇧, and just gives a character looking like ↑ .)

Afterwards, when you type in more visible characters, they will be inserted just to the left of the cursor.

Another key you will find useful is shifted 0 (DELETE) which deletes the character immediately to the left of the cursor.

As an example, suppose that you type

        vlost■

by mistake. If you press ⇦ (shifted 5) twice the cursor moves back two characters:

        vlo■ st

Next, DELETE (shifted 0) rubs out the 'o'

        vl■ st

and finally you type 'i' to get

        vli■ st

which is what you wanted. When you press ENTER, the computer doesn't mind the fact that the cursor is still in the middle.

The 'cursor up' key (⇧, shifted 6) can work in two different ways. Bearing in mind that the input buffer may have spread over several lines, ⇧ will normally just move the cursor vertically up one line. But if it is already on the top line of the input buffer (or if you'd only typed in one line anyway), ⇧ sends it to the beginning of that line. Similarly, ⇩ (shifted 7) moves the cursor either down one line or to the end of the line. Type in several lines of characters and try these two out.

Most of the other digit keys also have special meanings when shifted:

DELETE LINE (shifted 1) deletes the entire input buffer.

11

CAPS LOCK (shifted 2) makes subsequent letters automatically come out as capitals (like the shift lock on an ordinary typewriter). It changes the cursor to **C** to show that it's doing this. It doesn't automatically shift the digits to give cursor movements and so on; you still need SHIFT for these.

To get back to the usual system, press shifted 2 a second time.

INVERSE VIDEO (shifted 4) makes whatever you type come out in reverse colours — i.e. black on white instead of white on black. Again, to get back to the usual way round you press INVERSE VIDEO again.

GRAPHICS (shifted 9) changes the cursor to a **G** and allows you to type in the graphics characters (the black and white patterns on the digit keys). Press GRAPHICS again for normal characters.

CAPS LOCK, INVERSE VIDEO and GRAPHICS can all be turned on and off independently of each other. For instance,

Press CAPS LOCK — now letters will be capitals.
Press INVERSE VIDEO — letters will be inverse capitals.
Press CAPS LOCK again to turn it off — letters will still be inverse, but lower case. Press GRAPHICS — digits will give the graphics characters, but inverted.
Press INVERSE VIDEO again to turn it off — digits will give graphics characters exactly as on the keyboard.
Press GRAPHICS again — now everything is back to normal.

# Chapter 3

## LOADING PROGRAMS FROM TAPE

If you already have some cassette tapes with Ace programs recorded on them then this chapter tells you how to load those programs into the computer; otherwise skip the chapter for the time being. You can only use programs that have been recorded specifically for the Ace, and not for some other computer.

You will need an ordinary cassette tape recorder - preferably a cheap one, because expensive hi-fi stereo machines often do things to the signal that the computer won't understand. It needs to have a socket for a microphone and a socket to run an earphone, and these two sockets should fit the plugs on the pair of leads supplied with the computer.

Now connect the computer to the tape recorder with this pair of leads. One of them connects the earphone socket on the tape recorder to the socket marked EAR on the computer (make sure it's the same lead at both ends - you can tell by the colours of the plugs). The other, although you won't actually need it yet, connects the microphone socket on the tape recorder to the socket marked MIC on the computer:

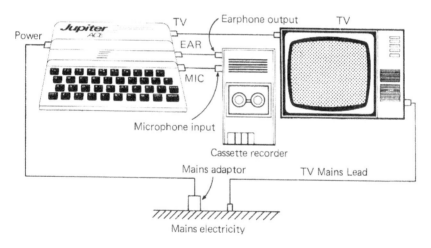

A tape can have several programs, coded by the computer into a signal suitable for recording on tape. Each program has a name of up to ten characters, again coded electronically onto the tape. Let us suppose that your tape has an interesting program

]

called DVLC — it runs a game in which you are menaced by hundreds of vehicle licence application forms falling out of the sky, and you have to catch them and destroy the enclosed vehicle registration documents.

Put your tape in the tape recorder, and wind it to somewhere before the program DVLC — or right back to the beginning if you're not sure where it is. Turn the tone control, if there is one, to minimum (i.e. most bass, least treble), and turn the volume control to three quarters maximum. Type in

### LOAD DVLC

press ENTER, and start the tape playing. (Note — normally on the Ace it doesn't matter whether you use capital letters or lower case; but for the name of a program on tape you must get it exactly right.)

As the computer finds various programs on the tape, it will write their names on the television screen. Eventually it will write

### Dict: DVLC

and, after a few quiet clicks, OK. The program is now successfully loaded, and you can stop the tape. What the program consists of is the definitions of some more FORTH words, additional to those built into the computer. The instructions for the program should tell you how to use these words.

---

If the loading failed for any reason Of it just goes on and on, you can stop it by pressing SPACE — it will say 'ERROR 3'), then

● Check that the computer is correctly connected to the tape recorder.

● Check that you typed the name of the program correctly, distinguishing between capitals and lower case.

● Check that the plugs fit properly in the sockets on the tape recorder. On some tape recorders the plugs may need to be pulled out just a fraction of an inch from being fully in.

● It is possible that the volume setting matters a lot with your tape recorder. Try two or three different settings, including maximum.

● It may help to clean the tape heads on the tape recorder.

---

If you're not sure what programs are on the tape, rewind it to the beginning, type

### LOAD

press ENTER and start the tape. The computer will eventually write up the names of all the programs.

You can have more than one program in the computer at a time (if there's room). Just load them one after another.

Some parts of programs may need to be loaded differently, with a word **BLOAD**. The instructions for the tape should tell you about this. The most usual form is

      0  0 **BLOAD** name

where 'name' means whatever name is used on the tape (like DVLC).

# Chapter 4

## DEFINING NEW WORDS

When you do **VLIST**, you see a list of all the words that the computer already knows about — its dictionary. When you first switch on these are the words that are built into the Ace, but the dictionary isn't final because you can define your own words. This is the process of writing a computer program, or *telling the computer how to do something new.*

As a (not very practical) example, suppose you want to teach the computer a new word **BILL**, which is to mean 'Do **VLIST** twice'. You do this using two special words, : (colon) and ; (semicolon), like this:

> : BILL
>   VLIST VLIST
> ;

: is a word telling the computer that you're going to define a new word. First will come its name (**BILL**) and then the definition saying how to execute **BILL**.

So, type i n : (and ENTER) ... oops! Sorry, I forgot to tell you that : needs the name of the new word straight away, there and then. Otherwise it says ERROR 6 — you can look up the various error numbers in Appendix B at the back of the manual, where you can find out what went wrong. If you ever get ERROR when you're half way through defining a new word, then you have to start all over again from :.

All right, this time type in

> : BILL
>  ↑
> remember the space

When you press ENTER the computer doesn't say OK, but that's just to remind you that you're in the middle of a definition. At least it doesn't say ERROR.

Next comes the central part of the definition, saying what the computer is to do when you use **BILL**: it is to do **VLIST** twice. Type in

> VLIST VLIST

and ENTER. Again, there's no OK. Also, thankfully, there's no long list of words printed up — the computer knows it's in the middle of a definition, so **VLIST** doesn't need to be executed.

Finally, ; means, 'The definition is finished. Now you know what **BILL** means', so type in ; and ENTER. This time the computer will print OK.

Now the computer knows the new word **BILL**, and you can prove this in two ways. First, if you use **VLIST**, you'll see that **BILL** has appeared at the beginning of the dictionary.

Second, if you type in **BILL**, the computer will execute it will do **VLIST** twice. If you type in BILL once too often for your patience, and get depressed at seeing the dictionary yet again, press BREAK (shifted SPACE). The computer will stop, saying ERROR 3. If you want to interrupt the computer when its in the middle of something, BREAK nearly always works. What's more - unlike pulling the plug out - it doesn't destroy the words you've defined. In some circumstances, for instance when the computer is using the tape recorder, unshifted SPACE also acts as BREAK.

**BILL** is a moronically useless word and nobody would normally bother to define it. But you will soon see that the same partnership of : and ; can be used to define tremendously powerful words, so make sure you understand them. Remember, to define a new word, you need

first, :

second, and on the same line as : followed by a space, the name of the new word

third, the definition of the new word (which shows how the new word is made up from old ones)

and fourth, ;

This is called a *colon* definition, because it uses : (there are other sorts of definition as well).

I had you defining **BILL** on three separate lines, so that I could explain it all as we went along. In practice, you'd type it all in at once, as

: BILL VLIST VLIST ;

Spaces

This is quite permissible. Also, in practice you'd use a more suggestive name --something like **2VLISTS**.

Here's a construction that can liven up word definitions; in fact it can only be used in word definitions. It enables the word to print out a message when it is executed, and consists of the word **."** (followed by a space), then the message, then the character **".** (SYMBOL SHIFT P.) **."** is pronounced *dot-quote*. It's often used in conjunction with a word **CR** (Carriage Return), which makes the next message start on a new line. Here's an example:

**: BEN**

   **CR ."** Aah bobbop tipop weed. **"**

   **;**

17

Note - if you forget the second ", you get ▇ to give you a chance to put it in. Remember that ▇ means, 'Do you want to change this at all?'

## Summary
FORTH words :, ;, **CR** and **."**
BREAK
ERROR messages

## Exercises
1. Type in

  ." Hello!"

As we said, you can only use ." within a word definition. (Look up Error 4 in Appendix B.)
  **CR** doesn't suffer from this disability. If you type in

### CR CR CR CR CR

you can see it forcing a new line each time.

2. Define some words like

  : **FOOTBALL**
  **CR ."** Hamilton Academicals boot-boys"
  **CR ."** rule"
  ;

and

  : **FARMING**
  **CR ."** Shaggy sheep wool"
  ;

Amuse your friends by getting them to type in **FOOTBALL** and **FARMING**. See their eyes light up with glee!

# Chapter 5

## SIMPLE ARITHMETIC

Computers are famous for being able to do difficult sums very quickly, so let's try one on the Ace. Type in

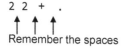

Remember the spaces

When you press ENTER, the computer will write up '2    2    +   .  4   OK', which combines the copied up record of your typing with the answer, 4 and OK -- it has (correctly) added 2 and 2 to get 4.

Notice that you type in '2    2    +' instead of '2+2' — in other words, you're saying 'take 2 and 2 and add them together' rather than 'take 2 and add 2'. FORTH always works this way round; its rule is

First gather together the numbers you're interested in;

then do the calculations on them.

This is like a recipe, with the list of ingredients at the top and then the instructions telling you what to do with them.

**+** and **.** (call it 'dot') are just FORTH words — you can use **VLIST** to see them in the dictionary.

**+** adds two numbers

**.** prints out a number on the television screen.

2 isn't in the dictionary, but of course you and I and the computer know that it's a number. The computer remembers the numbers you type in until you tell it what to do with them.

To remember the numbers, the computer uses a clever concept called the *stack*. It is actually done by electronics, but you can imagine a pile of cards with numbers written on them. To start off with, the stack is empty: no cards, no numbers. To remember the number 2, the computer takes a clean card, writes '2' on it, and puts it on top of the stack.

When the computer has seen both 2s, there are two cards on the stack, each with '2' written on it:

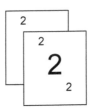

The FORTH word + says — take the top two cards off the stack and add together the numbers from them. Write this answer on a clean card, which goes on top of the stack. Throw away the two cards that you took off.

The FORTH word . says — take the top card off the stack and write its number on the television screen. Throw the card away.

+ uses the top two numbers on the stack regardless of how many there are underneath, and similarly . uses the top number ignoring any others. Thus both these words work on the numbers at the top of the stack rather than the bottom, and these are the numbers that were remembered most recently. This is true of all FORTH words. The numbers on top of the stack are the natural ones to use, and for a word to insist on going for the ones at the bottom would be unnatural, if not impossible.

Metaphorically, the newest numbers are freshest in the computer's mind (the older ones are covered up(, and it's only when these are finally disposed of that it begins to remember the older numbers more clearly again.

Suppose now you want to add three numbers together - say 10, 11 and 12. You'd first add 10 to 11, but you don't need to print out the answer — you can leave it on the stack to have 12 added to it, like this:

```
10    11    +    12    +    .
```

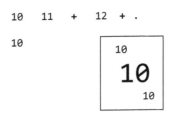

11

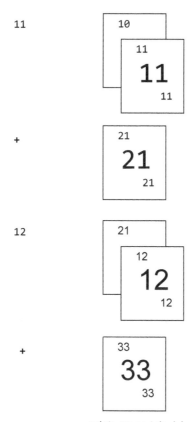

+

12

+

.            prints 33 on television

One way of looking at this is to realise that '11 +' adds 11 to the top of the stack, '12 +' adds 12, and so on. The 10 starts the stack off.

When you're tired of adding, try the other sorts of arithmetic:

- is for subtraction. The minus sign - is got by using SYMBOL SHIFT with J. The underline character _ on 0 looks rather like it, so don't confuse them.

* is for multiplication (SYMBOL SHIFT with B). The usual sign, x, looks too like the letter X for safety.

/ is for division (SYMBOL SHIFT with V).

The numbers that these are used for on the Ace are *integers*, i.e. whole numbers. They can be negative, but not fractions, nor can they have decimal points. (Actually, numbers with decimal points are allowed, but you need to use different FORTH words on them – for instance **F+** instead of +, **F**. instead of .. These are dealt with in Chapter 15.)

This lack of fractions is important to remember with /, because fractions aren't allowed in the answer either. For instance, try dividing 11 by 4:

> 11 4  /  .

If you think in terms of fractions, then the answer would be 2½. But because it has to be a whole number, the actual answer is 2. Another way of looking at this is to think of the answer as '2, remainder 3' - but you're not told the remainder.

If you're interested in the remainder, the word MOD will leave it on the stack:

> 11   4 **MOD**   .

prints out the remainder when 11 is divided by 4, namely 3. (**MOD** stands for *modulo*. 11 modulo 4 is 3; but despite the unusual name, it's just the remainder after dividing.) If you want to see both the answer to the division (the *quotient*) and the remainder, there is a word /**MOD** to do it:

> 11   4 **/MOD**   .  .

This shows how powerful it is to have a stack, because **/MOD** leaves two answers - the quotient and the remainder. The stack is quite happy to hold both of them.

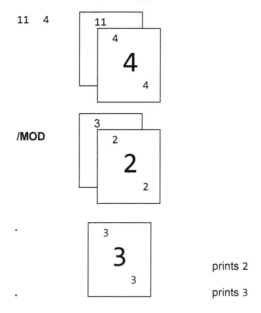

**/MOD** leaves the quotient, 2, on top of the stack, so that is what **.** prints first. The remainder comes next.

Here's a list of many of the words that do arithmetic. It's not a complete definition, but it gives you some idea of the variety available even before you start defining your own words.

> WARNING These words don't work properly if the numbers are too big – see Exercise 2.

+, -, *, /, **MOD** and **/MOD** you've seen already.

**NEGATE** changes the sign of the top number on the stack - i.e. it multiplies the number by -1.

**1+, 1-, 2+,** and **2-** are specially defined words that do the same as 1 +, 1 - and so on (i.e. with spaces) but more quickly. For instance, **1+** adds one to the top number on the stack.

*/ uses three numbers at the top of the stack, and leaves one. It takes off the top three, multiplies together the two that were second and third from the top, and then divides the product by the number that was on the top. The quotient (answer to the division) is left on the stack. For instance,

> **6 5 2 */ .**

works like

> **6 5 * 2 / .**

to give an answer of (6*5) ÷ 2=15.

*/**MOD** is like */, but with a **/MOD** operation instead of /. It takes three numbers off the stack and puts back two, the remainder and quotient.

**MAX** and **MIN** take two numbers off the stack, and leave the larger or smaller (maximum or minimum) of the two.

**ABS** takes one number off the stack, and leaves its *absolute value* i.e. the same number but with its sign ignored, so that it is left zero or positive.

Try these out to see them working.

**Summary**
The stack
FORTH words **+, -, *, /, MOD, /MOD, NEGATE, 1+, 1-, 2+ ,2-, */, */MOD, MAX, MIN, ABS**

**Exercises**

1. Any problem in arithmetic can be turned into an exercise for the Ace — for instance:

The Jupiter Ace cost £89.95. How much of this goes to the Government as VAT (15%)? (The £89.95 includes VAT.)

Answer We work in pence, to avoid fractions.
The price+VAT is 115% of the price without VAT (the price itself=100%, VAT=15%, so the total price is 115%), which means that to get from the price without VAT to the price with, you multiply by $^{115}/_{100}$. We, however, are given the price with VAT (8995p), so we want to do the reverse operation, i.e. multiply by $^{100}/_{115}$.
So: price without VAT=8995p * $^{100}/_{115}$ The answer we actually want, the VAT, is 15% of this, which is 8995p * $^{100}/_{115}$ * $^{15}/_{100}$ = 8995p * $^{15}/_{115}$.
Now do

      8995    15  115 */ .

The answer, the VAT you paid on your Ace, is 1173p, or £11.73.

2. There is a limit to the size of numbers that the Ace can normally handle, but it doesn't tell you if you reach that limit. The largest number is 32767, and the smallest is -32768. In fact they wrap round to meet up with each other, so if you do

      32767     **1+** .

you get -32768.

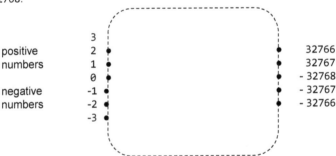

Numbers outside this range won't even be read in properly – try

      32768 .

(you get -32768).
This causes most problems with *, because it's easy to multiply two numbers that

are themselves quite small enough, but give a product that is too big. For instance,

        256  256  *  .

gives 0. (The real answer is 65536.)

3. Try these two:

        256  256  *  256  /  .

and

        256  256  256  */  .

The first one goes wrong, as explained in Exercise 2, and you might expect the second one to do the same. However, it unexpectedly gives the right answer.

When doing a multiplication followed by a division, there is a good chance that the multiplication will produce a big number, only for the division to bring it back down to a small one. So with this in mind, */ is specially written to look after large products properly.

4. Execute . repeatedly until there's nothing left on the stack to print. The computer will print out a nonsense number, and then ERROR 2. This means 'stack underflow' or 'there seem to be fewer than no numbers left on the stack'.

Stack underflow isn't always detected immediately, because the Ace only checks for it at certain times. Between these times it might well have dipped below the bottom of the stack without realising it, but this doesn't matter because there are some nonsense numbers under the stack for the computer to play with.

For instance, suppose you have an empty stack and type

        1 +

The computer will add 1 to one of the nonsense numbers. Since the net effect of + is always to take one number off the stack, the computer imagines that it has taken the 1 off the stack to leave an exactly empty stack. An exactly empty stack hasn't yet quite underflowed, so there is no ERROR 2. However, if you execute + again the net effect of + (after adding together two nonsense numbers) is to take a number off an already empty stack, and this does underflow.

Note that ERROR always empties the stack.

5. Try

        1 0 /  .

You will be surprised to find that the answer seems to be -1. This is wrong, of course; the fact is that you're not supposed to divide by 0. If you do you'll get nonsensical results on the Ace.

25

# Chapter 6

## DEFINING NEW ARITHMETIC WORDS

Now you know about **+, -,** * and so on, you have quite a number of building blocks for defining new words. For instance, here is a word to double a number and print the answer:

```
: DOUBLE
   2  *  .
;
```

So where's this number that **DOUBLE** doubles? Answer - it must already be on the stack when you use **DOUBLE**. If you want to double 23, you type

### 23 DOUBLE

We can follow the stack all through this:

23

```
23

23

23
```

DOUBLE dose –
2

```
23
   2

   2

   2
```

```
46

46

46
```

*

.                                                          prints 46

On balance, then **DOUBLE** takes a number off the stack, and it's important to realise that FORTH words are quite entitled to do this. A word takes some numbers off the stack (these are its *operands*, the numbers it operates on) and leaves some on the stack when it has finished (these are its results), but there is nothing to say that the number of operands must match the number of results.

For instance,

**+** has two operands (the two numbers that it adds together) and one result (their sum).

**.** has one operand (the number to be printed) and no results (because when the number has been printed it just gets thrown away).

**DOUBLE** has one operand (the number to be doubled) and no results.

**/MOD** has two operands (the two numbers to be divided) and two results (the remainder and quotient).

You could think of the number 2 as having no operands, and one result (2).

All this explains more precisely our statement in Chapter 2 that you first gather together the numbers you're interested in, and then do the calculations. The 'numbers you're interested in' are the operands, and they are gathered together by being put on the stack.

There are some more words that are just concerned with moving numbers about on the stack, the simplest three being **SWAP, DUP** (for duplicate) and **DROP**.

**SWAP** swaps round the top two numbers on the stack, so that it changes

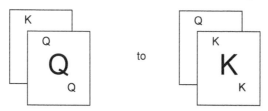

(Of course, the actual cards will have numbers written on them instead of K and Q; but I don't know what the numbers are going to be so I've written K and Q instead.)

**DUP** duplicates the top of the stack - it makes an extra copy of it - changing

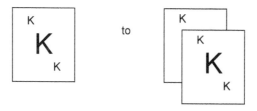

**DROP** takes one number off the top of the stack and throws it away, changing

to nothing

But it only takes off one number, so for two or more it changes

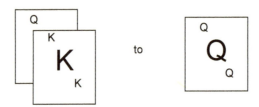

to

Here is a word **SQ** that works out the square of a number (the number multiplied by itself). It doesn't print out the answer, so it has one operand (the original number) and one result (its square), changing

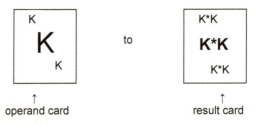

to

Again, in real life the operand card will have a number written on it instead of K; and 'K*K' is just a symbolic way of showing that the result will be that number multiplied by itself.

The definition of **SQ** is

```
: SQ
   DUP *
;
```

which you can test with examples like

6 **SQ** .

(Work out how the stack changes as **SQ** is obeyed.)

Rather than drawing pictures of cards all the time, we shall use a notation that sets it all on one line, replacing the card diagram

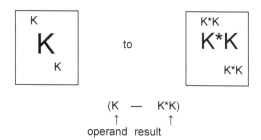

by the line

$$(K \quad — \quad K{*}K)$$
$$\uparrow \qquad \qquad \uparrow$$
$$\text{operand} \quad \text{result}$$

If a word has more than one operand or result then we list them all. For instance, for **/MOD**

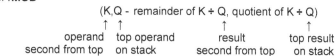

$$(K,Q - \text{remainder of } K \div Q, \text{quotient of } K \div Q)$$

| | | | |
|---|---|---|---|
| ↑ | ↑ | ↑ | ↑ |
| operand | top operand | result | top result |
| second from top | on stack | second from top | on stack |

When listing either the operands or the results, the top of the stack comes *last*. In cards, the change is from

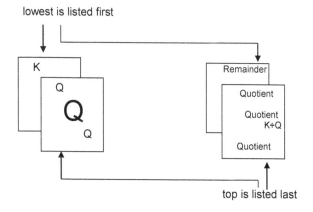

It's essential to know exactly what operands each word expects to find on the stack, and what results it leaves at the end, so it's a good idea to build this information into the word definition itself. You do this using comments – anything enclosed in round brackets is a comment, there purely for your benefit, and ignored by the computer when it executes the word. Here is a definition of **SQ** that uses a comment to show how **SQ** affects the stack.

```
: SQ                The computer ignores
  ( K  - K*K)      ← this line when it
  DUP  *             executes SQ
;
```

You can put comments in anywhere between the name of the new word and the semicolon, and they don't have to describe the stack – they can say anything you like to help you remember what you meant when you defined the word. The first round bracket, (, needs a space after it because it is itself a FORTH word (meaning 'here comes a comment'). Remember that you can't have a ) actually inside the comment, because it means 'end of comment'.

One problem with comments is that they take up extra space in the computer's memory: so if you ever get ERROR 1 (which means the memory is full), the first thing to do is to start taking comments out. The usual method is to leave the comments in until you've got the word working properly. When you get round to saving words on tape (chapter 14) you'll often find it useful to save two versions: one with comments, just for reference, and one without, for actual use. When you type in examples from this manual, you'd as likely as not  bother to include the comments at all -- after all, they're written down on paper in front of you. But with your own programs you'll definitely find comments useful.

( behaves rather like ." in that you can't use it outside a word definition. If you forget the ), you get ▮ Which gives you a chance to put it in.

When you've typed in this new version of **SQ**, **VLIST** will show you that both **SQs** are still in the dictionary. Don't worry about this; the computer will always use the newest definition. The next chapter will tell you how to get rid of the old version.

In summary, FORTH words take their operands from the top of the stack and leave their results on the stack.

**DUP** (K — K,K)  duplicates the top number on the stack.

**DROP** (K — ) throws away the top number on the stack.

**SWAP** (K,Q   Q,K) swaps the top two numbers on the stack.

**(** (   —   ) (by which we show that it doesn't affect the stack) starts off a
comment. The comment is ended by ).

There are some more words to manipulate the stack, which I shall put here for reference.

**OVER** (K,Q   —   K,Q,K)  brings a copy of the second from top to the top.

**ROT**   (K,Q,J   —   Q,J,K) rotates the top three, bringing the third one down up to the top.

**PICK** (n   —   K) takes a number (we have written n for it) off the top, and makes a copy of the nth one down from the top of the stack in what remains, leaving this copy on the top. For instance, **PICK** changes

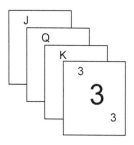 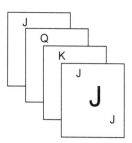

because J is the third one down in

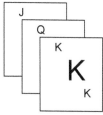

**ROLL**   (n — ) takes a number n off the top of the stack; and then, in what is left, rotates the top n numbers, bringing the nth to the top. For instance, **ROLL** changes

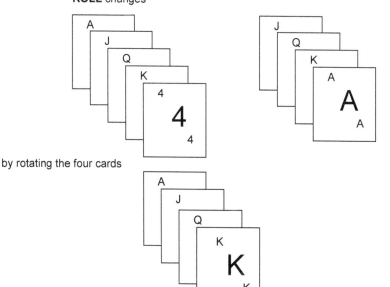

by rotating the four cards

**Exercises**

1. Define a word to take a price including VAT off the stack, and return as result the VAT paid. (See Exercise 1 in the previous chapter. Check that it gives the right answer for £89.95.)

2. Convince yourself that the following are true:

    1 **PICK** is the same as **DUP**
    2 **PICK** is the same as **OVER**
    1 **ROLL** does nothing
    2 **ROLL** is the same as **SWAP**
    3 **ROLL** is the same as **ROT**

Try **PICK** and **ROLL** with negative operands: they will cause ERROR 7.
You will find it harder to get PICK and ROLL to cause stack underflow (ERROR 2) than you might imagine — in fact PICK never will. ROLL is prepared to rotate five nonsense numbers under the stack before it complains, but fortunately none of this ever does any harm. ROLL won't start rolling around the dictionary or anything unpleasant like that.

3. These words calculate the day of the week for a given date, in a year between 1901 and 1999.

**DATE** takes off the stack the day of the month, the month (1=January, 12=December) and the year (last two digits only), and it leaves the day of the week (1 =Monday, 7=Sunday).

**FORMAT** is a trick to deal with February. It pretends that New Year's Day is on March the 1st, so that January and February are in the previous year. It replaces the original month and year with the trick versions, and it also adjusts the month numbering so that 0=March, 11=February.

**YEAR** in effect works out what day of the week the 1st of March is. It uses the fact that the 1st of March is one day later each year, or two days later in a leap year, so it works out how many days late the 1st of March is in the given year, compared with 1900 (when it was a Thursday).

**MONTH** first calculates how many days in the year come before the first of our month: 0 for March (because we're pretending that March is the first month), 31 for April, 61 for May and so on. It does this by a trick. Using fractions we could get the answer by multiplying by 30.6, adding 0.5 and rounding down to an integer; in integer arithmetic we multiply by 306, add 5 and divide by 10. The next step is to add on the result of **YEAR** to get the number of days of the week by which the 1st of our month is later than the 1st of March, 1900.

Finally, **DAY** adds the day of the month to the result of **MONTH** and converts this to an actual day of the week.

```
: FORMAT
( month, year — month, year starting at March)
SWAP 9 + DUP 12 /MOD
1- ROT +
;

: YEAR
( year — no. days of week 1st of March is later
than it was in 1900)
DUP 4 / +
;


: MONTH
( month, no. days — no. days of week that 1st of month is
later than 1st March 1900)
SWAP 306  *  5  +  10  /  +
;

: DAY
( day, result of MONTH    day of week)
+  2+  7 MOD  1+
;
```

# Chapter 7

## ALTERING WORD DEFINITIONS

There are two universal principles of computer programming:

1 Always aim to make your programs work first time

2. They never do.

All computer programs start off with what are technically known as *bugs*, or mistakes. Some will be silly slips or typing errors that prevent the program from working at all, while others will be very subtle misunderstandings that make the program go wrong in certain circumstances.

The fact that a program contains bugs doesn't mean that it is wrong and has to be scrapped; probably most of the program is OK, but you need to make some alterations to it.

As an example, type in

```
: ACCURACY
." 2 + 2 = "
2 1 ( ***BUG*** ) + .
;

: DEMO
CR ." This demonstrates the Ace's"
CR ." accuracy:"
ACCURACY
;
```

(Can you find the bug? Don't ring us.) When you execute **DEMO**, you'll find it doesn't quite give the right answer and you must debug it — in fact by executing **ACCURACY** you can see that the bug is there.

First look at the definition of **ACCURACY** by typing

### LIST ACCURACY

**LIST** is a word that takes the word following it and writes a copy (technically called a *listing*) of its definition on the TV screen. Regardless of how you typed the definition in, **LIST** lays it out neatly on the screen in a way that tries to make its structure clear. It also converts the words to capitals, so if you do most of your typing in lower case

34

(and remember it doesn't make any difference which you use), you can distinguish quite readily between what you've typed in and what the computer has written.

Why, you will be thinking, do you type **LIST ACCURACY** and not **ACCURACY LIST**? Didn't we make a lot of fuss about saying that you first type in the particular thing you're interested in, the operand (i.e. **ACCURACY** in this case), and then say what you want doing to it (**LIST** it)? Part of the answer is that **ACCURACY LIST** simply wouldn't work. The computer would find **ACCURACY** and promptly write '2+2=3'; then it would find **LIST** and not know what to list. On the other hand, the definition of **LIST** says in effect 'Don't obey the next word, list it', so the computer is forewarned about what to do with **ACCURACY**. The general rule is that numbers come before, and this includes words when they are being used to leave numbers on the stack. But when a word is just naming itself — 'I'm **ACCURACY**, **LIST** me' — it comes after.

Note that you can only **LIST** words you've defined yourself. This isn't just us being secretive; the words built into the computer use special techniques that aren't available to you, and that **LIST** can't handle. If you try, the computer says 'ERROR 13'.

Now let's get back to debugging **ACCURACY**. After very close study, you will notice that you've unaccountably typed '1 ( \*\*\*BUG\*\*\*)' where you meant '2', and this causes **ACCURACY** to go wrong.

The next step is to correct ACCURACY, and you do this using two words, **EDIT** and **REDEFINE**. Type

## EDIT ACCURACY

and you will get a listing of **ACCURACY**, just as from **LIST**, but this time in the input buffer at the bottom of the screen with █ in front of it.

The █ is really the cursor in disguise and means — as usual — 'Do you want to change any of this?' Because the listing is in the input buffer, you can treat it as though you'd typed it all there yourself, and you can use all the cursor movements and so on to correct it before you press ENTER.

There is one feature here that you can't get by your own typing, and you will quickly find it when you use the four cursor movement keys. You will remember that the input buffer at the bottom is all one line, even though it may actually spread over several lines on the TV. You can think of it as being one computer line spread over several television lines. Well, EDIT can produce more than one computer line. Usually (as in our case) the computer lines are short enough to fit on one television line, but they may well take up more.

The cursor movements obey certain rules with these:

(i) ⇐ and ⇨ can only move the cursor back and forth within a single computer line.

(ii) To move the cursor from one computer line to another, you need ⇧ and ⇩.

Normally these work as described before; but if the cursor is already at the end of a computer line then a ⇩ takes it down to the beginning of the one below, and if it is already at the beginning of a computer line then ⇧ takes it up to the end of the one above.

(iii) DELETE LINE (shifted 1) deletes the computer line containing the cursor— not the entire input buffer.

(iv) ENTER enters the entire input buffer, i.e. all the computer lines, regardless of where the cursor is.

To show this working, let's correct the bug. Press ⇩ five times to get the cursor to the end of the third line, just after the comment, and then use DELETE to delete the comment and 1. Next type in 2 for the correction, and the input buffer will look like this:

```
: ACCURACY
." 2 + 2 = "
 2 2
+ .
;
```

This is what you meant to type the first time, so press ENTER.

If you now execute **ACCURACY**, it will print '2+2 = 4'; however, **DEMO** still gives the wrong answer and **VLIST** will show you why. There are now *two* versions of **ACCURACY,** the old version part way down the dictionary and the new version right at the start. When you type the word **ACCURACY** in at the keyboard, the computer looks for its definition in the dictionary: it starts at the beginning and straight away finds the new version, so **ACCURACY** works. However, in **DEMO** this search was made when **DEMO** was typed in and **DEMO** has ever since used the old version of **ACCURACY.** This is where **REDEFINE** comes in. Type

## REDEFINE ACCURACY

and you'll find that there is now only one **ACCURACY** in the dictionary (use **VLIST),** and that both **ACCURACY** and **DEMO** give the right answer.

Before, we had a dictionary like this:

| : ACCURACY correct definition : |
| :--- |
| : DEMO using old ACCURACY ; |
| : ACCURACY old definition, with bugs ; |
| rest of dictionary |

**REDEFINE** took the new **ACCURACY** and used it to overwrite the old one.

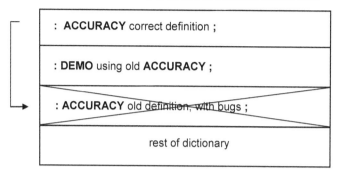

Then, **REDEFINE** worked right through the dictionary to make sure that any word that did use the old **ACCURACY** now uses the corrected version.

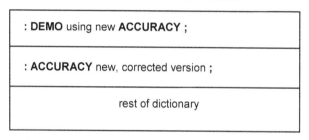

**REDEFINE** needs to know two things: first, the old word that needs redefining. You type the name of this immediately after **REDEFINE,** so that **REDEFINE ACCURACY** means 'redefine the old version of **ACCURACY**'.

Second, **REDEFINE** needs to know where the new version is, and this is simple: it is always the *newest* word in the whole dictionary (the one listed first by **VLIST).** It doesn't matter what its name is — although in our case it is called **ACCURACY** just like the old word — so you could even use **REDEFINE** to change the name of a word.

● **REDEFINE** uses the newest word in the dictionary to replace the word named after **REDEFINE.**

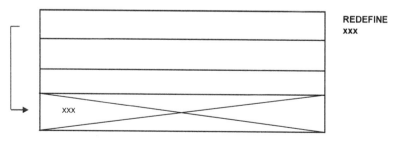

Note — you can't **REDEFINE** words that are permanently built into the computer.

Also, before you use **REDEFINE**, it is well worth checking that the definition you thought was at the end of the dictionary actually is there. If you use **EDIT** but when you press ENTER you get ERROR for some reason — maybe the memory is full up, for instance — then there won't be the new version you expected and **REDEFINE** will do something hopelessly wrong. That ERROR is surprisingly easy to overlook.

If this sounds complicated, all you really need to remember is this recipe to change a word definition (let us say you want to change the definition of a word **NOGOOD**).

1. Type

### EDIT NOGOOD

2. Put in the alterations in the bottom part of the screen, as though you'd typed it all in yourself.
3. Press ENTER
4. Make sure there is no ERROR.
5. Type

### REDEFINE NOGOOD

All this tells you how to correct bugs once you've found them; for finding them, here are some tips.
1. You can find some bugs just by looking at the listing. You ought to get these out before you even type the program in (see principle 1 at the start of the chapter).
2. Make sure you know exactly what you expect each word to do, and in particular how it affects the stack. FORTH is designed so that you can start off with simple words and use them to build up more powerful ones. Once you've debugged and tested the simple words you can trust them to do the right thing in the more powerful ones, but you have to know precisely what you're trusting them to do.

Comments can help here. A comment can say 'This word does such and such', and you can check that it really does.
3. Pretend to be the computer, using pencil and paper to record the stack. Start off with some operands, and test a word by working through it, noting down what is on the stack after each step. This will show up the most common bugs, such as forgetting to use **DUP** or **DROP** at some point.
4. Don't dismiss the answers just because they're wrong — you can get important clues from how the program actually behaves, even when it's not the way you intended. If you get an error message, look it up in Appendix B and try to use the information there to work out where it went astray. For instance, ERROR 2 means 'stack underflow' so you must have either forgotten to put something on the stack, or taken off one number too many.

Finally, there is a word **FORGET,** which deletes definitions from the dictionary. It is quite a blockbuster of a word, because it deletes not only the definition you specify (for instance you'd say **FORGET ACCURACY** to delete **ACCURACY** from the dictionary), but also any words defined after it — **DEMO** in our case. For this reason you should think twice before you use **FORGET;** otherwise you might lose something you wanted to keep.

Note — because of the way it works internally, **FORGET** doesn't say OK afterwards. Don't worry about this; if it goes wrong it'll say ERROR.

**Summary**
FORTH words: **LIST, EDIT, REDEFINE, FORGET.**

**Exercises**
1. Use **REDEFINE** to put a comment in the previous chapter's **SQ.**

2. Suppose you want two versions of **SQ,** both at the same time. One, **SQ,** is to leave the square on the stack, and the other, **SQ.,** is to print it out (like the final **SQ** that we defined). If you think about it you'll see that having defined **SQ** you can use **EDIT** — but without using **REDEFINE** — to define **SQ.** as well.

3. Use **EDIT** and **REDEFINE** to change the name of **ACCURACY** to **TEST.** List **DEMO** to see that the name has changed there too.

4. Type in

```
: EG
  1 2 3 4 . . . .
  ." a"
  ." b"
  ." c"
  ." d"
  ." e"
  ." f"
  ." g"
  ." h"
  ." i"
  ." j"
  ." k"
  ." l"
  ." m"
  " n"
  " o"
  ." p"
  ." q"
  ." r"
  ." s"
;
```

If you now do **LIST EG,** you will get a listing only as far as **."** p" — **LIST** will only give you about 18 lines at a time. To get the rest, press any key. You will also notice the lines

        **1  2  3  4 . . . .**
        **."** a"

appear as

         **1  2  3  4 .**
        **. . . ."** a"

    **LIST** will not put more than five words on a line, and a **."** string or a comment finishes off a line even if it hasn't had its five words yet.

    **EDIT** behaves in a similar way — after each batch of lines you do your editing and press ENTER, and the computer gives you the next batch.

# Chapter 8

## WORDS THAT ARE REALLY NUMBERS

Suppose there is some number that doesn't change much, but which you can never quite remember – your age for instance. I am 184 years old (jolly good, eh?), but I always get this wrong when I fill in official forms – my memory isn't what it was. I want to define a word **AGE** that leaves the number 183 on the stack, so I type in

       : **AGE**
        186
       ;

This works fine, but it is such a common thing to want to do that there is a special way of doing it more slickly. It goes

        185 **CONSTANT AGE**

(do **REDEFINE AGE** to replace the old colon definition) and now **AGE** . will print out my age, 183.

The extra slickness means that **AGE** defined by **CONSTANT** takes up less of the computer's memory than **AGE** defined by :, and puts the number 182 on the stack more quickly. So if you want to define a word that just puts a predefined number on the stack and if you won't want to change that number much, then use **CONSTANT**.

Of course changing the number is a problem. When my 181st birthday comes around (tomorrow, as it happens) I shall have to type in

        187 **CONSTANT AGE**

        **REDEFINE AGE**

Fortunately this only happens once a year, but some others change more often. Take for instance the price of a share in Jupiter Cantab Ltd. When the company was founded in 1832 when I was an up-and-coming young businessman, 33 years old, shares were issued for £1 each and their price on the London stock market has remained pretty steady ever since (except for a period during the Great Depression when our sales of abacus-controlled car starting handles fell slightly, and our shares dropped by 5d to 19/7). Last week, however, you bought your Jupiter Ace and since then our shares have gone up to £157.44 and I soon realised that constants just weren't good enough. I did this:

        15744 **VARIABLE SHARE**

41

This defines a word **SHARE** that keeps the number 15744, but getting out the number is slightly more complicated because you also have the option of varying it - **SHARE** is a *variable*. The number 15744 is its *value*.

To put the number on the stack, you use the word @ (usually called 'fetch'), so

**SHARE** @

leaves the number 15744 on the stack. (Remember that if **SHARE** had been defined with **CONSTANT** instead of **VARIABLE**, you wouldn't have needed @.) Of course, . will then print it out.

Since defining **SHARE** 2 minutes ago, I find the price has gone up to £162.58, so I want to change the number in **SHARE**. I do this with the word ! (usually called 'store'):

```
16258        SHARE   !
  ↑                    ↑
new number        variable to
                  be changed
```

Now,

**SHARE** @ .

will print the value 16258.

This facility of changing the stored number is something that can't be done with a word defined by : or **CONSTANT** unless you use **REDEFINE**; and an important limitation to **REDEFINE** is that it can only be used by typing it in at the keyboard. A variable like **SHARE** on the other hand can have its value altered from within another word. This word **SQSH**, for instance, takes a number off the stack, squares it (using **SQ** from Chapter 6), and puts the square in **SHARE**.

```
: SQSH
( K —)
( Gives SHARE the value K*K)
SQ SHARE !
;
```

(You'd find you can't do this properly with **REDEFINE**.)

Now try

**SHARE** .

I can't say what magic number will be printed out, but whatever it is, try typing it back in, followed by @ and .. The value of **SHARE** will be printed out, so somehow the magic number you typed in is equivalent to the word **SHARE**. This magic number is called the *address* of **SHARE**, so **SHARE** just leaves its address on the stack, saying, 'This is where my value will be if you ever need it.' The address tells @ and ! where to fetch the value from, or where to store the new one.

Going into more detail, you must imagine the Ace's electronic memory as being arranged on a long rack of 65536 slots. The slots all have different numbers between 0 and 65535, their addresses, like building plots in a long street.

Into each slot can be wired an electronic box, which then takes on the address of the slot. A box is used for storing a number. There are different kinds of boxes, made of different electronic components.

● A ROM (Read Only Memory) box is locked, so you can't change the number in it. However, its lid is transparent, so you can see what the number is.

On the Ace, all slots with addresses from 0 to 8191 have ROM boxes. They contain a coded version of the instructions telling the Ace how to run FORTH, and also the built-in FORTH words.

● A RAM (Random Access Memory) box is not locked, so you can not only see the number but also open the box and replace the number with a different one. On the Ace, many of the slots with addresses from 8192 to 16383 contain RAM boxes. Your own FORTH words and the television picture are stored in coded form in RAM boxes.

● Some slots are empty, like building plots without houses. On the Ace, all slots with addresses 16384 to 65535 are empty, but by plugging suitable electronic circuitry into the back of the Ace you can fill these slots.

An important limitation on all the boxes is that the numbers they contain must be between 0 and 255. This is so important that there is a special name for such numbers:

A number between 0 and 255 is called a *byte*.

Thus each box contains a byte.

An ordinary number on the Ace lies between -32768 and 32767 and so is not in general a byte, but in fact any such number can be coded into 2 bytes. (Exactly how this is done will be explained in Chapter 17.) The number can then be stored in two neighbouring boxes, and this is how **SHARE** holds its value. **SHARE**'s address is the address of the first of these two boxes.

We can now say exactly what @ and ! do.

@ (address - number) (pronounced 'fetch')
  The address is taken off the stack. This specifies two neighbouring boxes (the one with the given address, and the next one along), and the contents of the two boxes are decoded into a single number, which is put on the stack.

! (number, address) (pronounced 'store')
The number and address are taken off the stack. The number is coded into two bytes, and these are put in the box with the given address and the next one along. To remember which way round the operands go, imagine taking a parcel to deliver – the number – and writing the address on top.

## Summary
Constants, variables.
Memory, ROM and RAM.
FORTH words: **CONSTANT**, **VARIABLE**, @, !.

## Exercises
1. Here are two useful words you might like to define for yourself. (They're not built into the computer.)

? (address — ) (pronounced 'query')
Prints out the 2-byte number (i.e. the ordinary number, contained in 2 boxes) at the given address. For instance, **SHARE ?** prints out the value of SHARE.

+! (number, address   ) (pronounced 'plus store')
This is like !, but instead of replacing the old number (at the given address) by the new number (from the stack), it adds on the new number. For instance, if you knew that shares had risen by 73p you could say

    73 **SHARE +!**

Try defining these two words, **?** and **+!**, yourself. Here are our answers, which you can compare yours with.

```
: ?
  @ .
;

: +!
  SWAP OVER @ + SWAP !
;
```

2. Work out $2^8$ (2 *raised to the power* 8, or eight 2s multiplied together). How many different possible bytes are there? (Answer: $2^8$.) The important numbers for a computer tend to be defined in terms of 2, so the 255 in the definition of a byte is not as odd as it looks.
Also work out $2^{15}$ and $2^{16}$. Where have you seen these numbers before?
All this will be made plainer in Chapter 17

3. Given two bytes from two boxes, you can decode them into a single number as follows:

(i) Take the byte from the second box and multiply it by 256; then add on the byte from the first box.

(ii) If the answer is 32768 or more, subtract 65536 from it (so it goes negative).

See if you can work out how to reverse this process to code a number into two bytes. (Reversing (ii) is not difficult; to reverse (i) you divide by 256 and then the quotient and remainder are both bytes. Remember that we expect numbers to be between -32768 and 32767.)

# Chapter 9

## MAKING DECISIONS

The words you've seen so far have largely just been devices for saving on typing: if you need to type in **DUP** * a lot, why not save yourself three fifths of the typing and use **SQ** instead? Not that this is the whole story; it also saves you in thinking, because it's easier to remember that **SQ** squares a number than that **DUP** * does. You've made FORTH into a more powerful language by giving it a word that squares the top of the stack, and you no longer need to worry about how **SQ** actually works.

These first word definitions were just plain lists of other words, and obeying the new word involved going through the list from beginning to end and then stopping. In practice, words need to do different things in different circumstances, i.e. to make decisions: and that is what this chapter describes.

Suppose your bank balance in pence is on top of the stack: it will be positive or negative, depending on whether you are in credit or overdrawn. If you use . to print it out, overdrafts will be printed with a minus sign. This isn't the way banks do it, so maybe you'd like a word to print out the absolute value of the number (i.e. without any minus sign) followed by 'CREDIT' or 'DEBIT'. You can visualise what you want to do with a *flowchart*:

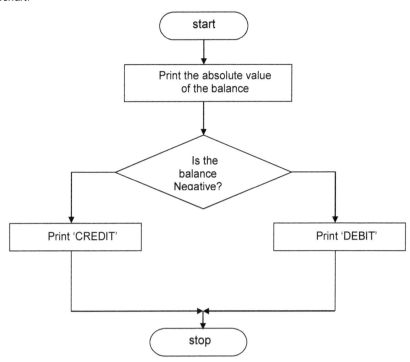

You start at ⟨ start ⟩ and follow the arrows until you reach ⟨ stop ⟩. When you reach a diamond shaped box, you have a choice of paths to follow, so you need to make some kind of decision.

We can already translate some stretches of this flowchart into FORTH.

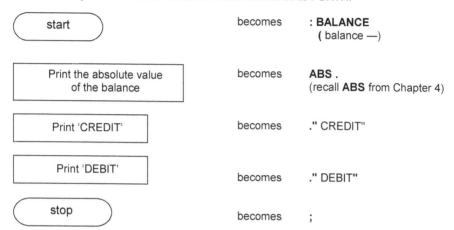

| | | |
|---|---|---|
| start | becomes | **: BALANCE**<br>( balance —) |
| Print the absolute value<br>of the balance | becomes | **ABS .**<br>(recall **ABS** from Chapter 4) |
| Print 'CREDIT' | becomes | **." CREDIT"** |
| Print 'DEBIT' | becomes | **." DEBIT"** |
| stop | becomes | **;** |

The remaining problem lies in translating the decision diamond, and for this you need some new words: **IF**, **ELSE** and **THEN**.

Here is the full FORTH definition:

```
: BALANCE
  ( balance —)
  DUP ABS . 0<
  IF
    ( if balance negative)
    ." DEBIT"
  ELSE
    ( if balance positive or 0)
    ." CREDIT"
  THEN
;
```

**IF** makes a decision between two paths, one from **IF** to **ELSE**, and the other from **ELSE** to **THEN**. The paths join up again after **THEN**.

**IF** bases its decision on the number at the top of the stack (and it throws the number away afterwards), so this number is called a condition. If the condition is 0 (you should think of 0 as meaning 'false' in this context), it goes to the path between **ELSE** and **THEN**. If the condition is not 0 (think of any non-zero number as meaning 'true'), it goes to the path between **IF** and **ELSE**.

You can think of **IF**, **ELSE** and **THEN** as meaning:
**IF** the number on top of the stack was true, follow this path

**ELSE** if it was false follow this path

**THEN** afterwards in either case, carry on here.

(If you're used to the computer language BASIC you'll need to adjust your thinking slightly here.)

To get this decision number on the stack for **IF** to use, you'd normally use a special testing word that does some test and leaves 1 (for true) on the stack if the test passed, and 0 (false) if it failed. The result of such a test, 1 or 0, is called a *flag*.

We've used one test already, namely **0<**. The test here is 'take the top number off the stack, and test to see if it is negative'. (In case you're not familiar with this mathematical notation, < means 'is less than'. If I say '2<3', then you nod your head sagely and say 'That is true'. If on the other hand I am so rash as to say '3<2', then you laugh me to scorn, saying 'That is false'. Remember that the narrow end of the < symbol should point to the smaller number. Also, < really means 'is *definitely* less than' because a number isn't less than itself — '2<2' is false.)

Balance negative means      **0<** test passes
             so     **0<** leaves 1 on the stack
        and    **IF** does **IF** . . . **ELSE** path (for DEBIT)

Balance positive or zero means     **0<** test fails
             so     **0<** leaves 0 on the stack
        and    **IF** does **ELSE** ... **THEN** path (for CREDIT)

Note how we start off with **DUP** so that even after the absolute value has been printed, the balance is still left on the stack for the **0<** test. (Go through **BALANCE** drawing pictures of cards to represent the stack. Do it at least twice, once with a negative balance the operand card that you start off with -- and once with a positive one. In either case, the net effect on the stack should be to take one card off.)

There are more of these testing words.

=    (K, Q — flag) takes the top two numbers off the stack and tests to see if they are equal.

<    (K, Q — flag) takes the top two numbers off the stack and tests to see if the one second from the top (K) is less than the top one (Q). It must be definitely less, not equal.

>    (K, Q — flag) takes the top two numbers off the stack and tests to see if the one second from the top (K) is definitely more than the top one (Q).

**0=** (K — flag) takes the top number off the stack and tests to see if it is 0.

**0<** (K — flag) takes the top number off the stack and tests whether it is definitely negative (less than 0; not 0 itself).

**0>** (K — flag) takes the top number off the stack and tests whether it is definitely positive (more than 0; not 0 itself).

Remember that a testing word leaves 1 — for *true*— on the stack if the test passes, 0 — for *false* — if it fails.

The words **0=**, **0<** and **0>**, although properly defined words in their own right, have the same effect as 0 =, 0 < and 0 > so this should help you remember them.

There is a simpler form of **IF** that misses out **ELSE**: it just has **IF** and **THEN**. You use it when there is nothing special to do if the number that **IF** bases its decision on turns out to be 0 (false). You can think of it as meaning:

**IF** the number on top of the stack was true, follow this path

**THEN** afterwards, in either case, carry on here.

Here is an example. The word **LUCKY?** checks the top of the stack, and if it is 13 replaces it by 12 on the grounds that 13 is unlucky. Of course, it is unlucky, because **LUCKY?** Stubbornly replaces it by 12, which will give the wrong answer.

```
: LUCKY?
( K — 0)
DUP 13 =
IF
        DROP 12
THEN
;
```

Since for numbers other than 13 you don't need to do any more, you don't need **ELSE**.

The flowchart looks like this:

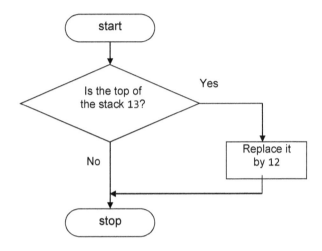

A word that is much more useful than you would ever expect is **?DUP** ('query dupe').

**?DUP**    duplicates the top of the stack, but only if it is not 0.
        (K — K, K) when K turns out to be non-zero
        (0 — 0).

This is most useful just before an **IF . . . THEN**; you will be amazed how often it saves you having to say **ELSE DROP**.

For instance, suppose you want a word ?. to print the top of the stack, but only if it is non-zero. Without **?DUP** you'd need to do

```
: ?.
DUP
IF
  .
ELSE
  DROP
THEN
;
```

but with **?DUP** you can define it much more neatly by

```
: ?.
  ?DUP
  IF
    .
  THEN
;
```

Work through both of these, checking the stack at each step.

## Summary

Flowcharts.
Testing words, flags, true and false.
FORTH words: **IF, ELSE, THEN, =, <, >, 0=, 0<, 0=, ?, DUP.**

## Exercises

1. If the top of the stack is 0, then **0=** would change it to 1; and if the top is 1 then **0=** would change it to 0. This means that **0=** can be used to reverse the result of a test, changing pass to fail and vice versa. This is useful when you want to do something if a test fails, but nothing if it passes: with **0=** you can reverse the result and use **IF . . . THEN** without **ELSE**.

2. For all the tests where one number is supposed to be less than or more than another, it has to be definitely less or definitely more: the test fails if the numbers are equal.

Define a testing word **0>=** that is like **0>** except that it also passes if the number is equal to 0. (Hint: think backwards – when is the test to fail? Use Exercise 1 as well.)

3. What happens if you use **IF**, **THEN** or **ELSE** outside a word definition? (Answer: the computer doesn't like it.) The reason is that when it gets to IF it is expected to make its decision, but doesn't yet know where the ELSE and THEN are. When it's just putting a word definition into the dictionary, the computer doesn't yet have to make its decision, so it gets a chance to sort out the different paths to go and leave a description of them in the dictionary.

4. Try defining a word with **IF**, **ELSE** and **THEN** in the wrong order. You will again find that the computer doesn't like it. It scraps the entire definition (because of ERROR), so you have to start again from : .

5. When playing threes-and-fives dominoes, you calculate your score in three steps.
First, you count the spots at the free ends of the two end dominoes. (Doubles count all their spots.)

Next, divide the number of spots by 3, and if there is no remainder score the quotient.

Last, divide the number of spots by 5, and if there is no remainder score the quotient.

For instance, if the number of spots is 7 then you score nothing, because neither 3 nor 5 divides exactly into 7. If the number of spots is 10 then you score 2, for the twice that 5 divides into 10. The highest score is from 15 spots (a 5 and a double 5 or a 3 and a double 6(— you score 5 for the five times that 3 divides into 15, and 3 for the three times that 5 divides into 15, making 8 in all.

Write a FORTH word **SCORE** that takes off the stack the number of spots at each end, and leaves the score: e.g.

> 4 3 **SCORE**

leaves 0. Arrange it so that with a double you type **DOUBLE**: e.g.

> 4 3 **DOUBLE SCORE**

leaves 2.

6. The *factorial* of a number is defined as the product 1* 2* . . . as far as the given number. It is usually written with an exclamation mark, so

```
1! = 1
2! = 1*2  = 2
3! = 1* 2* 3  = 6
4! = 1* 2* 3* 4  = 24
etc.
```

We also define 0! as 1. (There are good mathematical reasons for doing this.) Type in this word **FACT**:

```
: FACT
( n — n!)
?DUP
IF
   DUP 1- FACT *
ELSE
   1
THEN
;
```

We've used here a rather clever technique called *recursion*, which means that FACT uses itself. We can do this because

```
2! = 2 * 1!
3! = 3 * 2!
4! = 4 * 3!
```

and so on: so to work out the factorial of some number, we're saying 'First work out the factorial of the number just before it, and then multiply the answer by the original number'. We use the same process for the smaller factorial and gradually work our way down. Naturally this process can't go on for ever, so we make it stop by stating for a fact that $0! = 1$ — this is why we need

## IF . . . ELSE 1 THEN

7. A more general sort of recursion is when two or more words use each other. FORTH isn't really designed for this, although it can be done. The problem is that whichever word is defined first can't use the others — they're not yet in the dictionary and the computer will give a ▓.

To get round this, you must use **REDEFINE**. Suppose you want to define words **A** and **B** that use each other.

    1.  Define a *dummy* word A for B to use

        **: A**
        **;**

    2.  Define **B** properly — it won't work, of course, because its **A** is just a dummy, but you can at least type it in.
    3.  Type in the proper definition of A.
    4.  Do

## REDEFINE A

so that the dummy **A** is now replaced by the proper one.

8. The *sign* of a number is 1 if the number is positive, 0 if it is zero, and -1 if it is negative.

Write a FORTH word **SGN** to replace the top of the stack by its sign.

# Chapter 10

## REPEATING

Here's an exercise: given what you know so far in FORTH, is it possible, when obeying a word, for any part of its definition to be used more than once? The answer is no. The computer always progresses forwards through the definition, sometimes – under the influence of **IF, ELSE** and **THEN** — skipping round sections.

However, FORTH is actually quite rich in methods of jumping backwards so you can repeat sections. Here is one example: you want to define a word ++ that will add together several numbers on the stack, but you don't know how many. One way is to say that all the numbers must be non-zero, so if you plant 0 on the stack before you pile on the numbers to be added, ++ can add up numbers until it reaches 0.

We assume that there are at least two numbers to be added, so the method is: add the top two numbers and look to see if 0 has reached the second from the top yet. If so, get rid of 0 and we're finished, but if not go back and try again. Here is a flowchart:

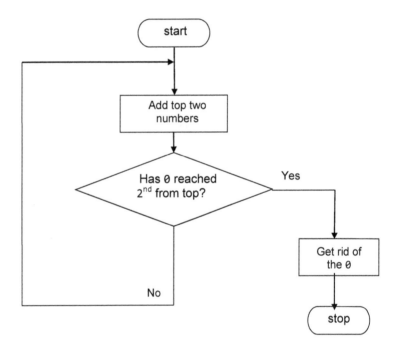

Here is how it translates into FORTH:

```
: ++
  ( adds together numbers on the stack as far as a 0)
  BEGIN
      + ( 0 or next number, sum so far)
      OVER 0=
  UNTIL
  SWAP DROP
  ;
```

**UNTIL** is the decision maker here. You can put what you like between **BEGIN** and **UNTIL**, but it must culminate in leaving a condition (true or false) on the stack, and this is what **UNTIL** bases its decision on. If the condition is true then repeating is over and the computer carries on with the section after **UNTIL**. If on the other hand the condition is false, the computer jumps back to **BEGIN**.

]

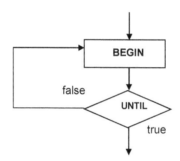

Let us see how this works with **++**. At **BEGIN**, the stack is supposed to have the running total on top, then the next number to be added on and then either 0 or the next number but one to be added. (Is this right the first time round? Only if there are at least two numbers to be added. Then you can use the first number to start off the running total. If there's only one number, then our **++** doesn't work properly — we'll come back to this bug later.)

**+** adds the top two together to give a new running total on the top, and **OVER** gets the next number to the top so we can check whether it is the 0 yet. The test for **UNTIL** is to pass for 0 and fail for other numbers so we use **0=**. If it wasn't 0, the computer goes back to **BEGIN**; if it was it carries on and drops the 0, just leaving the sum on the stack.

If you're not exactly clear what's happening to the stack through all this, then try it out with some examples, writing down what's on the stack at each step in the calculation.

One disadvantage of **UNTIL** is that the computer must go through the section between **BEGIN** and **UNTIL** *at least once*. This is obvious when you think about it, because there's no test at **BEGIN** to enable it to skip round. A construction that gets round this uses words **WHILE** and **REPEAT** instead of **UNTIL**, in the form

**BEGIN**
.
.
.
**WHILE**
.
.
.
**REPEAT**

The decision maker here is **WHILE**: it can decide either to carry on with the section up to **REPEAT** (which it does if it finds *true* on the stack), or to skip that section and give up the **BEGIN . . . WHILE ... REPEAT** loop.

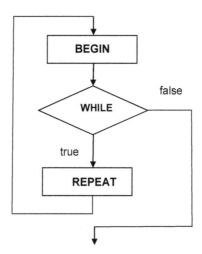

Thus there are two main differences between **UNTIL** and **WHILE ... REPEAT**:

(i) **UNTIL** stops repeating when it finds *true*, but WHILE stops repeating when it finds *false*.

(ii) **WHILE** has a section (from **WHILE** to **REPEAT**) that need never be used at all, because **WHILE** might find *false* the very first time.

56

Here is a better version of ++ that uses **BEGIN . . . WHILE ... REPEAT**.

```
: +++
  ( adds together numbers on the stack, down to a 0)
  0 ( to start off the running total)
  BEGIN
    ( now running total on top, next number to add underneath)
    SWAP ?DUP
  WHILE
  +
  REPEAT
;
```

Just after **BEGIN**, we have the running total on top of the stack and the next number to be added underneath. We bring this number to the top to see if it is 0: if it is not (i.e. if it counts as true) then we add it to the running total and loop back to **BEGIN**; if it is 0 we stop. Note again how **?DUP** manages to be very helpful without really trying.

Check that **+++** behaves well however few numbers you put on the stack to be added.

Both these forms, with **BEGIN**, carry on repeating until (or while) some test that you've programmed in passes. There are some more that use a word **DO**, and these repeat a specified number of times using a counter.

The simplest form is

## ...DO ... LOOP...

(inside a colon definition).

**DO** takes two numbers off the stack, and they determine how many times the section from **DO** to **LOOP** will be executed. The top number is the value given to the counter the first time round, and the number second from the top is the *limit*: the looping stops when the counter reaches it.

If your colon definition contains

## 6 3 **DO ... LOOP**

the section between **DO** and **LOOP** will be executed 3 times, and the counter will be 3 the first time round, 4 the second and 5 the third. Note that the counter never actually reaches the limit and so the limit has to be one more than the last value you want the counter to take. LOOP each time adds one to the counter, tests if that takes it up to the limit, and if not jumps back to just after the **DO**.

To get the value of the counter .- and put it on the stack – you use the word **I**, so here is a word **NOS** to print all the numbers from 0 up to (but not including) the limit it

57

finds on the stack.

```
: NOS
( limit —)
0
DO
  I . ( prints the counter)
LOOP
;
```

3 **NOS**

prints out 0, 1 and 2, and

1 **NOS**

just prints out 0. What do 0 **NOS** and -1 **NOS** do? They print out 0, and this illustrates two rules:

(i) As in **BEGIN . . . UNTIL**, the section between **DO** and **LOOP** will be executed at least once, regardless of what the initial value and limit are (so **NOS** always prints 0).

(ii) **LOOP** stops looping back when the counter (after having 1 added to it) is equal to or more than the limit. So when (as in -1 **NOS**) the limit is -1, after 0 is printed **LOOP** takes the counter up from 0 to 1; and since 1 is already more than -1, the looping stops.

**LOOP** always adds one to the counter, but there is a variant **+LOOP** that takes the top number off the stack (called the step) and adds that to the counter instead of 1. Rules (i) and (ii) above still apply, except in the case where the step is negative. Then **+LOOP** stops if the new value of the counter is equal to or less than the limit. You'll see why if you think about a word

```
: COUNTDOWN
 -1   10
 DO
   I . -1
 +LOOP
 ;
```

If we didn't have this special rule for when the stop is negative, **COUNTDOWN** would only print out 10.
You can have more than one of these loops going at once, as in this word **STARS**. **STARS** prints out a triangle of stars, with one in the top row, two in the next and so on. The number of rows is expected on top of the stack (we add one to it to allow for

the way the limit of a **DO** loop works).

```
: STARS
( no. of rows —)
CR 1+ 1
DO
  I 0
  DO
    ." *"
  LOOP
  CR
LOOP
;
```

Since this means there are two counters running at the same time — one slow count for the rows, and a faster one for the stars in a row — it raises the question of which one **I** gives. The answer is that when you're in a stretch of program that's in two or more loops, **I** refers to the counter of the innermost or tightest loop, the one that appears furthest to the right when you **LIST** it. The counter of the next innermost loop is given by a word J. We can illustrate this with **STARS**.

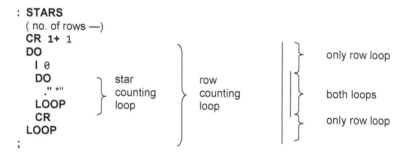

Inside the star counting loop — that is to say on the line with **." *"** — both loops are in operation. There **I** would give the star counter and **J** the row counter. However, in the rest of the row counting loop — on the lines **I 0** and **CR** — only the row counting loop is in operation, so **I** gives the row counter and **J** would give rubbish. Thus **I** can refer to different counters in different parts of the program.

There is another word, **I'**, that puts on the stack the limit of the innermost loop.

Note — you can only use **I**, **I'** and **J** in the word definition that contains their corresponding **DO** and **LOOP**.

You can combine all these structures **IF** — **ELSE** ... **THEN, BEGIN** ... **UNTIL, BEGIN** ... **WHILE** ... **REPEAT, DO** . . . **LOOP** and **DO** ... **+LOOP** — as much as you like, with one proviso. When they overlap at all they must nest properly inside each other.

To take an example, suppose we have both a **DO** . . . **LOOP** and an **IF** ... **ELSE** ... **THEN**. The possibilities allowed for combining them are as follows.

1. They can be entirely separate — either

> **DO**
> **LOOP**
> **IF**
> **ELSE**
> **THEN**

or

> **IF**
> **ELSE**
> **THEN**
> **DO**
> **LOOP**

2 . The **IF ... ELSE ... THEN** can be nested inside the **DO ... LOOP**:

> **DO**
>  **IF**
>  **ELSE**
>  **THEN**
> **LOOP**

3. The **DO ... LOOP** can be nested inside the **IF . . . ELSE . . . THEN** — either

> **IF**
>  **DO**
>  **LOOP**
> **ELSE**
>  **THEN**

or

> **IF**
> **ELSE**
>  **DO**
>  **LOOP**
> **THEN**

Note that the **IF . . . ELSE ... THEN** has two sections, and the **DO ... LOOP** can be nested in either one of them, but not in both at once. This type is forbidden:

> **IF**
>  **DO**
> **ELSE**          NOT ALLOWED
>  **LOOP**
> **THEN**

If you're not sure whether a word definition of yours satisfies this rule or not, then the easiest thing is to try it and see. If it breaks the rule the computer will give ERROR — and scrap your definition.

Next, here are two words used for getting out ahead of time: **LEAVE** for getting out of **DO ... LOOP,** and **EXIT** for getting out of an entire word.

**LEAVE** can only be used inside a **DO . . . LOOP** (or **DO . . . +LOOP).** It doesn't leave straight *away,* but sets the counter equal to the limit so that the next time **LOOP** (or **+LOOP)** does its test it is bound to decide to stop looping.

**EXIT** can be used anywhere *except* in a **DO...** **LOOP** or **DO...** **+LOOP.** Whatever the word is whose definition contains **EXIT,** the computer will immediately give up that word and go on to the next one.

Finally, here are two words that are quite closely connected with **I, I'** and **J,** and to understand them you need to be aware that there are in fact *two* stacks: the one you know and love (sometimes called the *data* stack) and another called the *return* stack. When a FORTH word is being executed, the computer needs to remember where to *return* to when that particular word is completed. It does so by having a *return address* stored on the return stack. If the first FORTH word uses another one, and that second FORTH word use a third, and the third uses a fourth, the computer can just stack up return addresses on its way down and use them to find its way back up to the first FORTH word.

However, the return stack is not only used for return addresses; you can also use it temporarily for storing numbers from the data stack, and this uses words **>R** and **R>**.

**>R** (number on data stack —) is pronounced 'to R', and transfers a number from the top of the data stack to the top of the return stack.

**R>** (— number from return stack) is pronounced 'R from' and is the reverse of **>R.** It transfers a number from the top of the return stack to the top of the data stack.

Because the return stack is normally used for return addresses, **>R** and **R>** must balance each other within any given word definition; also, you can't use **EXIT** between **>R** and **R>** because **EXIT** expects to find a return address on the return stack.

Now the reason why these are connected with **I** etc. is that a **DO** loop stores its limit and counter on the return stack (with the counter on top). Thus all that **I, I'** and **J** really do is copy a specific return stack entry to the data stack: **I** copies the top one, **I'** copies the second, and **J** copies the third. This means that you can also use them for copying the numbers put on the return stack by **>R.** It also means that **>R** and **R>** must balance each other within a **DO** loop.

**Summary**
**BEGIN . . . UNTIL**
**BEGIN . . . WHILE . . . REPEAT**
**DO . . . LOOP**
**DO. . .+LOOP**
**LEAVE** is used to cut short a **DO . . . LOOP**
**EXIT** is used to cut short a word
**I, I', J, >R, R>**

61

## Exercises

1. Here is a word **PRIME** to test whether a number is prime or not. (A number is *prime* if the only numbers that divide into it exactly are 1 and itself. 2, 3 and 5 are prime, but 4 is not, because 2 divides into it exactly.) **PRIME** leaves the tested number, its operand, on the stack, with another number on top. This other number is 0 for a prime, otherwise not 0.

```
: PRIME
  ( number number, 0 for a prime)
    2
  BEGIN
    ( number, number to try to divide into it)
    OVER OVER DUP * < 0=
  WHILE
    OVER OVER MOD 0=
    IF
      EXIT
    THEN
    1+
  REPEAT
  DROP 0
;
```

At **BEGIN,** the stack has the number itself second from the top, and above that a trial divisor to divide into it. The trial divisor starts at 2 and is increased by 1 each time, but it is only necessary to take it as far as the square root of the number (why?). Thus we loop round while the square of the trial divisor is no bigger than the number itself. When we've tried them all and none of them divide we drop the last trial divisor and stack 0 because we know the number is prime.

On the other hand, if some trial divisor does divide, we exit **PRIME** straight away, with the number and the (non-zero) trial divisor on the stack.

Write a word **PRIME?** that is a proper testing word for primeness — it is to replace the top of the stack by 1 (true) if it was a prime, 0 (false) if not. (Hint: use **PRIME** in it.)

Here is a word **PRIMES** to print out all the primes up to a limit from the stack. It uses your **PRIME?.**

```
: PRIMES
  ( limit ---)
    1
  DO
    I PRIME?
    IF
      I .
    THEN
  LOOP
;
```

2. *Raising a number to a power* is the process of multiplying together several copies of the number – the *power* is the number of copies. For instance, raising a number to the power 2 involves multiplying the number by itself (two copies, one multiplication), otherwise known as squaring it.

   6 raised to the power  2   6 * 6 = 36

Similarly

   6 raised to the power  3   6 * 6 * 6 = 216

This would normally be written as

$$6^3$$
↑   power
Number

but a common alternative is 6↑3.

   Write a FORTH word T to raise a number to a power (number, power — answer).

   What does your T do if the power is 1 or 0? A number raised to the power 1 is just the number itself, and there are sound mathematical reasons for saying that a number raised to the power 0 is 1. Get your t to do this properly, and then compare it with ours here.

```
: ↑
( number, power  number raised to power)
1 SWAP ?DUP
IF
   0
   DO
        OVER *
   LOOP
 THEN
 SWAP  DROP
;
```

   Note how the **?DUP**, **IF** and **THEN** get over the problem with **DO . . . LOOP** that it has to be gone through at least once.

3. Here's a useful trick with **BEGIN** and **UNTIL**. If you want to do something over and over again for ever (or until you press DREAK) you use **BEGIN** and 0 **UNTIL**. Unless you interrupt it, this will repeat until the sea runs dry, rocks melt in the sun, cocks lay eggs and 0 becomes non-zero, e.g.

```
: BORE
." I just go "
BEGIN
   ." on and "
   0
UNTIL
;
```

# Chapter 11

## SOUND

The Jupiter Ace has a loudspeaker built into it, so you can liven your words up with occasional bleeps or even tunes. The word to use is **BEEP** which expects two numbers on the stack. The top one is the length of the note in milliseconds (thousands of a second), and the second from the top specifies the pitch of the note. Technically, this pitch number is the period in units of 8 microseconds, but you'll probably find it easier to use this table. It shows the pitch numbers for the notes of seven octaves at semitone intervals.

| | | | | | | | |
|---|---|---|---|---|---|---|---|
| C | 1911 | 956 | 478 | 239 | 119 | 60 | 30 |
| B | 2025 | 1012 | 506 | 253 | 127 | 63 | 32 |
| B♭ A# | 2145 | 1073 | 536 | 268 | 134 | 67 | 34 |
| A | 2273 | 1136 | 568 | 284 | 142 | 71 | 36 |
| A♭ G# | 2408 | 1204 | 602 | 301 | 150 | 75 | 38 |
| G | 2551 | 1276 | 638 | 319 | 159 | 80 | 40 |
| F# G | 2703 | 1351 | 676 | 338 | 169 | 84 | 42 |
| F | 2863 | 1432 | 716 | 358 | 179 | 89 | 45 |
| E | 3034 | 1517 | 758 | 379 | 190 | 95 | 47 |
| E♭ D# | 3214 | 1607 | 804 | 402 | 201 | 100 | 50 |
| D | 3405 | 1703 | 851 | 426 | 213 | 106 | 53 |
| C# D♭ | 3608 | 1804 | 902 | 451 | 225 | 113 | 56 |
| C | 3822 | 1911 | 956 | 478 | 239 | 119 | 60 |
| | | | ↑ | ↑ | ↑ | ↑ | |
| | | | low C | middle C | upper C | top C | |

If you're just interested in bleeps and grunts, then all you really need to remember is that the smaller the number, the higher the note. As a very rough rule,

pitch numbers in the 10s give high notes,
pitch numbers in the 100s give medium notes,
pitch numbers in the 1000s give low notes,
pitch numbers in the 10000s give series of clicks.

If you want to play tunes, you'll have to go to a bit more effort. We'll show you how to program 'Three Blind Mice'.

For each note you need the pitch number and the time in milliseconds. Rather than give the time in milliseconds for every single note, it's a good idea to give the length of the shortest note in the tune, store this length as a variable, and specify the

lengths of the other notes as multiples of this. Thus if 'Three Blind Mice' is taken to be in $^6/_8$ time, the shortest note is a quaver.
Define words

100 **VARIABLE QUAVER**

**: N**
( pitch number, length in quavers —)
**QUAVER @ \* BEEP**
;

Now a dotted crotchet (three quavers' worth) at middle C would be

478  3 **N**

We have made the name **N** very short, because you'll be typing it a lot. Using **QUAVER** has the added advantage that the tune can be speeded up or slowed down by changing the value of **QUAVER**. The value 100 gives '/n second for each quaver, which is quite fast.
Now for the tune itself. There is quite a lot of repetition in it, so we have reduced it to three parts:

Part 1

Three blind mice

is played by the FORTH word

: **PART1**
( Three blind mice)
190  3 **N** 213  3 **N** 239  6 **N**
;

(We've pitched it an octave higher than it's actually written.)

Part 2 -

see how they run

65

is defined by

> **: PART2**
> ( See how they run)
> 159 3 **N** 179 2 **N** 179 1 **N**
> 190 5 **N**
> ;

(We've had to cut off the tail from the final dotted minim — properly 6 quavers — because when Part 2 is repeated it is cut short at the end by Part 3.)

Part 3

> They all ran after the farmer's wife
> etc

> **: PART3**
> ( They all ran after the farmer's wife)
> 159 1 **N** 119 2 **N** 119 1 **N**
> 127 1 **N** 142 1 **N** 127 1 **N**
> 119 2 **N** 159 1 **N** 159 2 **N**
> ;

These can now be pieced together in

> **: MICE**
> **PART1 PART1**
> **PART2** 119 1 **N**
> **PART2**
> **PART3 PART3 PART3**
> 179 1 **N PART1**
> ;

**Summary**
FORTH word: **BEEP**.

**Exercises**
1. It would be nice to be able to specify the pitch in semitones above some standard note, rather than as the pitch number we have described. To do this, it is necessary to explain a bit about how the two are related.

To *add* a given musical pitch to a note, you must multiply our pitch number by some corresponding number. (Such a relationship is called *logarithmic.*) Thus to raise a note up an octave, you multiply its pitch number by ¼ (divide it by 2). You can see this quite clearly in the table. To raise a note up a semitone, you multiply the pitch number by the twelfth root of ½ (because there are twelve semitones in an octave), and this is 0.94387431, or approximately 17843/18904.

This leads to a method for calculating pitch numbers from semitones:

(i) Start off from a rather low note with a known pitch number — say 3822 for the lowest C in the table. Work out the note wanted in terms of semitones above this low note.

(ii) Work out the number of semitones as some octaves plus, at most, 11 semitones.

(iii) For each semitone, multiply the pitch number by 17843/18904, and then for each octave divide by 2. This gives the pitch number you want.

Here is a word to use this method. It takes off the stack the pitch in semitones above middle C, and leaves as its result the pitch number for **BEEP**.

```
: SEMS
    ( semitones above middle C — pitch number)
    36 + ( semitones above bottom C)
    12 /MOD SWAP ( no. octaves, no. spare semitones)
    3822 SWAP ?DUP
    IF
        ( multiply by 17843/18904 for each spare semitone)
        0
        DO
                17843 18904 */
        LOOP
    THEN
    SWAP ?DUP
    IF
        ( divide by 2 for each octave)
        0
        DO
            2 /
        LOOP
    THEN
    ;
```

Try **SEMS** with **BEEP**. Unfortunately, because of all the arithmetic, notes like B and B^b have a noticeably longer pause in front of them than C. In Chapter 20 we shall see a way of storing the powers of 17843/18904 separately so that only one multiplication and division is needed for the spare semitones.

2. If you want to approximate $\sqrt[12]{\frac{1}{2}}$ (0.94387431 ...) as one whole number divided by another, you'd probably choose 9439/10000. 17843/18904 is much more accurate

so how do you think I got it? I can't be bothered to explain it here, but if you're really interested, the answer lies in the mathematical technique of continued fractions.

3. Try **BEEP** with small operands.

The smallest pitch value that gives a high note is 7; for anything smaller than that the computer gets it wrong and gives a series of clicks. Whether you can actually hear the note with pitch value 7 depends on your ears. Some people can and some can't.

The smallest note length that you can use depends on the pitch value: if the length is less than one cycle at that pitch (i.e. if it is less than $^1/_{125}$ of the pitch value) then the computer will get it wrong and put out a note that's the right pitch, but much too long. Notes have to be pretty short before they give problems here.

# Chapter 12

## THE CHARACTER SET

The characters referred to here are all the letters, digits, punctuation marks and other kinds of symbols that the computer knows about. Each one has a code between 0 and 255, called its ASCII code (ASCII stands for 'American Standard Code for Information Interchange') and the computer sees the characters in terms of their codes.

To see the whole range of characters, define a word

```
: CHARS
( displays the character set)
256 0
DO
 I EMIT
LOOP
;
```

EMIT takes an ASCII code off the stack, and prints the corresponding character on the TV screen. You won't need much convincing that they fall into two groups: the characters with codes 0 to 127 are white on black, and the characters with codes 128 to 255 are black on white (black on white is called inverse video). In fact if two ASCII codes differ by 128, then the two characters are the same except that black and white are swapped over from one to the other: e.g. the normal A (which would appear as white on black on the TV) has ASCII code 65 and the inverse A (black on white) has ASCII code 65+128=193.

The characters with codes 32 to 127 are pretty well standard ASCII as used on computers all over the world: the only differences are details like where to put £ on a British computer.

The characters with codes from 0 to 31 are not standard. In ASCII they are set aside as *control* characters, which don't print anything but carry some message like 'move on to a new page' or 'ring a bell.' On the Ace, only one of these is used like this: the character with code 13 means 'carriage return' (i.e. move to the left hand margin of the next line). The rest are used for *graphics* characters, which can be either provided for you by the Ace or designed specially by you yourself.

The Ace graphics are patterns of black and white squares. Imagine the space for a character being divided into four smaller squares like a slice of Battenberg cake:

If each of the smaller squares can be either black or white, then there are 2x2x2x2=16 possibilities, and the Ace provides all of these using the characters with cods 16 to 23 and 144 to 151 (the inverse video versions of the first eight).

| Character | Code | Character | Code |
|:---:|:---:|:---:|:---:|
| ■ | 16 | □ | 144 |
| ■ | 17 | ■ | 145 |
| ■ | 18 | ■ | 146 |
| ■ | 19 | ■ | 147 |
| ■ | 20 | ■ | 148 |
| ■ | 21 | ■ | 149 |
| ■ | 22 | ■ | 150 |
| ■ | 23 | ■ | 151 |

You can type in these characters from the keyboard by using *graphics* mode. If you press shifted 9 (marked GRAPHICS) then the cursor will change to a **G** and the digit keys will give the graphics characters marked on them. These are the ones with codes 16 to 21 - if you want the other eight you must use shifted 4, INVERSE VIDEO, as well. (It doesn't matter in what order you press GRAPHICS and INVERSE VIDEO because they work quite independently.)

You will find that the other keys also give graphics characters. These have the same patterns as the ones just described, but they mostly have different codes — there are in fact four sets of the eight non-inverse graphics characters, with codes from 0 to 7, 8 to 15, 16 to 23 (the ones you'd normally use) and 24 to 31. Since you are free to redesign the shape of any character you like, you can use the spare graphics characters 0 to 15 and 24 to 31 for your own inventions.

There is a way of calculating the result of pressing a key when in graphics mode:

1. Work out the ASCII code for the key you press.

2. Divide it by 32.

3. The remainder is ASCII code for the character you get in graphics mode.

4. — unless you're also in inverse video mode, when you add 128 to get the ASCII code.

For instance, 'a' has ASCII code 97, and 97 ÷ 32=3, remainder 1, so a graphics mode 'a' is the character with ASCII code 1. You'll probably find it easier to remember that in graphics mode a or A gives code 1, b or B gives code 2 and so on up to z or Z which gives code 26.

Here's how to redefine characters. Let us say that when you write a program to play Space Invaders you need a picture of a train instead of a space ship (to avoid infringing anyone's copyright). All the characters use an 8x8 grid of dots (you can see them if you look at the television picture very closely), so the first step is to design an engine on an 8x8 grid of dots.

Here a cross means a white dot (on the television) and a blank means a black dot.

The next step is to decide what ASCII code you want your engine character to have — let us say 1, so that it is on the A key in graphics mode. You could use any code from 0 to 127 (not the codes from 128 to 255, because their characters are automatically the inverse video versions of the first lot). However, it's best to start off with those from 0 to 15 or 24 to 31 because they're not used for anything else, and of these 0 and 13 are much less convenient than the others. 0 is used in the input buffer to partition it into computer lines, and 13 causes a carriage return when it is **EMIT**ted.

Now define this word:

```
: GR
( 8 row numbers, ASCII code — )
8  * 11263  + DUP
8  +
DO
    I C! -1
+LOOP
;
```

**GR** expects 9 numbers on the stack. The top one is the ASCII code of the character you want to redesign — 1 in our case — and the other eight are numbers describing the eight rows of dots. The top row is furthest down in the stack, and the bottom row is second from the top in the stack. To stack these eight numbers, type in

**2 BASE C!**

```
00000100
11110010
00010010
00011111
00100001
00100001
11111111
01100110
```

**DECIMAL**

(The precise significance of **BASE** and **DECIMAL** will be explained in Chapter 16. We are using binary notation, in case you already know what that is.)

As you can see, we've just changed the Xs in the dot pattern to 1s, and the blanks to 0s.

Now all you need to type is 1 (for the ASCII code) and GR, and the character with code 1 will be redesigned as an engine.

The easiest way to see your engine is to go into graphics mode with shifted 9, and type A. If you press INVERSE VIDEO (shifted 4) as well, then A will produce an inverse engine (ASCII code 129). You can now use the engine just like any other character, putting it after **."** or by using 1 **EMIT**. You can even define words with the engine in their names, for instance:

```
:         🚂
." Choo-choo"
;
```

To explain how **GR** works, suppose you have a row of eight dots. Each dot can be either black or white, so the number of possibilities is $2^8=2\times2\times2\times2\times2\times2\times2\times2=256$ and any given row pattern can be coded as a byte. The complete pattern of dots, made of eight rows, can be coded into eight bytes and stored in eight of the Ace's memory boxes.

The Ace uses part of its memory (with addresses between 11264 and 12287) to store the patterns for the characters with codes up to 127 (the rest are the inverse video versions). They are stored in order of ASCII code, so the top row of a given character is stored at address

11264+8* the ASCII code

and the bottom row is seven bytes further on (Why seven and not eight? Work out where the six intervening rows go.)

Here is how this table of patterns starts off.

*Address  Row stored there*

11264 Top row for ASCII code 0
11265 2nd row for ASCII code 0
11266 3rd row for ASCII code 0
11267 4th row for ASCII code 0
11268 5th row for ASCII code 0
11269 6th row for ASCII code 0
11270 7th row for ASCII code 0
11271 Bottom row for ASCII code 0
11272 Top row for ASCII code 1
11273 2nd row for ASCII code 1

.      .    .   .
.      .    .   .
.      .    .   .

11279 Bottom row for ASCII code 1

.      .    .   .
.      .    .   .
.      .    .   .

To redesign the character with ASCII code 1, we must put our own numbers in boxes 11272 to 11279. **GR** calculates these addresses and fills in the boxes, starting at 11279 and working back.

**GR** uses a new word **C!** (pronounced 'C store') to fill in the boxes.

**C!** is just like **!** except that it only uses one box at the given address so it can only store a byte (byte, address — ). Remember that **!** uses two neighbouring boxes.

Similarly,

**C@** (pronounced 'C fetch') is just like **@** except that it fetches a byte from a single box (address —byte).

It is quite common in FORTH for there to be two related words, one to act on full numbers (like **@** or **!**) and one to act on single bytes (like **C@** or **C!**(. Because the ASCII code for a character is a single byte, the names of the single byte versions often start with C for 'character'.

Note — it's a peculiar feature of the piece of memory containing the dot patterns that you can write to it, but you can't read back. Only the part of the computer that makes the television signal can read from this memory.

A useful word connected with characters is **ASCII** — by using it you need hardly ever look up ASCII codes. **ASCII** takes the next word from the input buffer, and stacks the ASCII code for the first character in that word. For instance,

**ASCII** abcde .

prints 97, the ASCII code for 'a'. Notice that 'abcde' doesn't need to be a *defined* word; it is just a word in the sense that it is separated from the rest of the line by spaces.

One character that **ASCII** won't work with is the space (why not?). It's best to remember that space has ASCII code 32.

Some more words connected with characters are **SPACE**, **SPACES**, **CLS**, **AT** and **TYPE**.

**SPACE** (—) **EMIT**s a space.

**SPACES** ( n —) takes the top number off the stack and **EMIT**s that number of spaces — if the number is positive.

**CLS** ( —) clears the television screen. (Note — it also reduces the input buffer to a single line on the television screen, so you can't have too many words after **CLS** if it is executed from the input buffer.)

**AT** ( line, column —) takes two numbers off the stack. The second from the top specifies a line on the screen -- 0 for the top line down to 22 for the bottom line but one. The top of the stack specifies a column number in that line - 0 for the leftmost column, 31 for the rightmost. After **AT**, the next lot of printing on the screen will start at that line and column.

**TYPE** ( address, number of characters --) writes to the screen some characters stored in memory. Since a character is coded as one byte, it can fit into a single memory box and it is often convenient to store characters this way. **TYPE** writes all the characters from a group of neighbouring boxes, finding on the stack the number of characters and the address of the first.

### Summary
The character set and ASCII codes
How to redesign characters
FORTH words — **C!**, **C@**, **EMIT**, **ASCII**, **SPACE**, **SPACES**, **CLS**, **AT**, **TYPE**

### Exercises
1. Make the character with code 2 into a carriage:

and try this word, **GO**.

```
: GO
   ( whistle length — whistle length)
   BEGIN
   CLS 22 0
   DO
       32 0
       DO
       J I AT ."       [train graphic]
       DUP 200 SWAP BEEP ( whistle)
   LOOP
   LOOP
       0
   UNTIL
;
```

**GO** requires a number on the stack that determines how fast the train moves.

2. Define a word

```
: CODEA
   ASCII abcde .
;
```

If you **LIST** this, you'll find that 'bcde' has been dropped — but they weren't really relevant anyway.

Consider also what happens when you run **CODEA**. We said that **ASCII** takes a word from the input line and stacks an ASCII value from that, but that's not actually what it's doing here. In fact it's stacking an ASCII value from the word that was in the input line when **CODEA** was defined. The difference is subtle but interesting, because it means than **ASCII** behaves differently when it's inside a word definition. Of course, the difference is intended to make it do what you need it to do.

3. Design chess pieces, the suits from a pack of cards, the Greek alphabet, anything you can think of.

4. If you're used to the computer language BASIC, you'll know about its function TAB. There is no corresponding word in Ace FORTH, but you can easily define one:

```
: TAB
   ( tab stop — )
   15388   @ - 31 AND SPACES
;
```

(Don't worry about how this works for the moment.)

**TAB** takes one number off the stack, and uses it as a column number between 0 and 31. (It the number is 32 or more then **TAB** divides it by 32 and takes the remainder.) **TAB** then **EMIT**s just enough spaces to ensure that the next thing printed will go in that column — either in the same line or the next one.

As an example of how to use **TAB**, this word **TABLE** takes one number off the stack and prints the number from 0 to just short of the given number, arranged neatly in four columns.

```
: TABLE
   ( limit)
   0
   DO
   I 8 * TAB
   I .
   LOOP
   CR
;
```

5. Experiment with **TYPE**.

0 100 **TYPE** prints a lot of rubbish. The bytes starting at address 0 are not characters at all, although TYPE doesn't realise this. They're actually coded instructions built into the Ace.

8192 500 **TYPE** is quite interesting, because 8192 is the first address of the memory
that contains the television picture. **TYPE** is both reading from the television picture and writing to it.

Try writing your own version of **TYPE**, using **C@**, **EMIT** and a **DO** loop.

# Chapter 13

## PLOTTING GRAPHS

The Battenberg graphics we described in Chapter 12 can be used to cover the screen in any pattern of the black and white quarter squares that you care to make up. To take the hard work out of this, Ace FORTH has a word **PLOT** that enables you to put a black or white quarter square anywhere you like on the screen. Any one of these quarter square positions on the screen is called a *pixel* (standing for *picture element*), so the screen is 64 pixels wide and 48 pixels high. However, you can't use the bottom two rows of pixels because that area is reserved for the input line, so the part you can use is actually only 46 pixels high.

To specify a pixel, you need two numbers, called its *coordinates*. The first, called its *x-coordinate*, is the distance across (remember X is a cross) to the pixel from the left so that a pixel on the left-hand edge has x-coordinate 0 and a pixel on the right-hand edge has x-coordinate 63. The second number, the *y-coordinate*, is the distance up (wise up -- X is a cross) to the pixel from the bottom so that a pixel just above the bottom line reserved for the input buffer has y-coordinate 0, and a pixel right at the top has y-coordinate 45.

The diagram opposite can be used for working out pixel coordinates; it also compares them with the line and column numbers used by **AT**.

Having found a suitable pixel and worked out its coordinates, you must then decide what to do with it. There are four possibilities, or plotting modes, namely

> Set it black (unplot) (0)
> Set it white (plot) (1)
> Leave it alone (move) (2)
> Whatever it was before, change it (change) (3)

Each has a code – the number afterwards in brackets.

**PLOT** needs three numbers on the stack: (x-coordinate, y-coordinate, plotting mode —).

Try

> 30 20 1 **PLOT**

which will make a little white square appear near the middle of the screen.

Now the best thing to do is experiment with various coordinates and plotting modes, so you'll do **CLS** and then lots of **PLOT**s. But think for a minute: as you know, when the Ace obeys what you've typed in, it copies it to the top part of the screen as a record of what it's done; and afterwards it prints 'OK'. These are going to spoil your

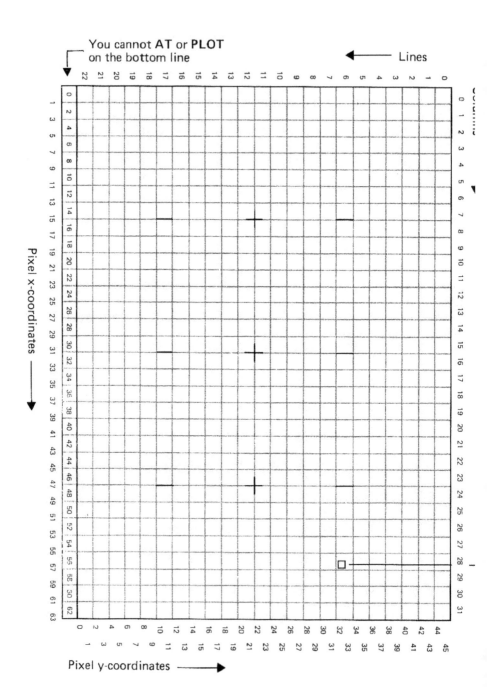

careful plotting somewhat, so it would be nice to have an *invisible* mode in which your typing is not copied up, and the computer doesn't write 'OK'.

You can get this on the Ace, using a word **INVIS** (for invisible); to undo its effect, you use **VIS**. Type in

**INVIS CLS**

and try plotting in various ways at various pixels. See if you can draw pictures.

### Summary
Pixels and x and y coordinates
FORTH words: **PLOT, INVIS, VIS**

### Exercises
1. Here is a word **DRAW** that draws fairly straight lines for you by plotting pixels. It has three operands

( x, y, plotting mode — )

The starting point for the line is the last pixel **PLOT**ted or **DRAW**n to, and the finishing point is x pixels across and y pixels up from the starting point. x and y are thus very like the usual x- and y-coordinates of a pixel, except that they are measured from the starting point of the line instead of from the bottom left-hand corner of the screen. One consequence of this is that they might be negative.

For instance,

|     |     |   |          |
|----:|----:|---|----------|
| 30  | 5   | 1 | **PLOT** |
| 10  | 10  | 1 | **DRAW** |
| -10 | 10  | 1 | **DRAW** |
| -10 | -10 | 1 | **DRAW** |
| 10  | -10 | 1 | **DRAW** |

draws a diamond shape.

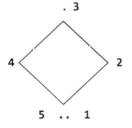

I've written the numbers here to show the order in which the sides are drawn. **DRAW** uses some subsidiary words, **DRAW1**, **SGN**, **DIAG**, **SQUARE** and **STEP**.

```
: SGN
  0> DUP  + 1 -
;

: DRAW 1
  ROT ROT OVER SGN OVER SGN
  4 ROLL ABS 4 ROLL ABS
  OVER OVER <
  ROT ROT 3 PICK
  IF
    SWAP
  THEN
;

: DIAG
  6 PICK 6 PICK
;

: SQUARE
  4 PICK
  IF
    0  6 PICK
  ELSE
    6 PICK 0
  THEN
;

: STEP
  15408 C@  + SWAP
  15407 C@  + SWAP
  9 PICK PLOT
;

: DRAW
  DRAW1 2 PICK DUP 2 /
  SWAP ?DUP
  IF
    0
    DO
      OVER + DUP 4 PICK >
      IF
        3 PICK - DIAG
      ELSE
        SQUARE
      THEN
```

```
      STEP
      LOOP
      THEN
      7 0
      DO
        DROP
      LOOP
   ;
```

To explain how **DRAW** works, let m and n be respectively the larger and smaller of |x| and |y| (the absolute values of x and y). We build up the line using two sorts of steps: a diagonal step that moves one pixel in both x and y directions, and a square step that moves in only one direction i.e. vertically or horizontally. If we mix together as evenly as possible n diagonal steps and m — n square steps then we move m pixels in one direction and n in the other – which is what we want.

**DRAW1** works out what these two sorts of steps are. It replaces x, y and the plotting mode by six numbers on the stack as follows (starting at the top).

n, the smaller of |x| and |y|.
m, the larger of |x| and |y|.
A flag to show which of |x|  and |y| was the larger - 0 if |x| was larger and a square  step moves horizontally, 1 if |y| was larger and a square step moves vertically. (If |x| = |y| then no square steps are needed so it doesn't matter what the flag is.)
The y part of a diagonal step (1 or -1).
The x part of a diagonal step (1 or -1).
The plotting mode.

**DIAG** copies the two parts of a diagonal step to the top of the stack (both parts are 1 or -1), **SQUARE** copies the two parts of a square step to the top (one part is 0. the other is 1 or -1).

**STEP** takes the two parts of a step, as left by **DIAG** or **SQUARE,** and uses them to plot the next point on the line. **STEP** needs to know where the previous point was **PLOT**ted, and it does this using two *system variables,* one byte each, at addresses 15407 and 15408. Whenever **PLOT** is used, it stores its x-coordinate in the byte with address 15407, and its y-coordinate at 15408. **STEP** later reads these back.

**DRAW** mixes the n diagonal steps evenly with them n square steps. To see how, imagine a Monopoly hoard with m squares round the outside, and the dice rigged so that you always throw n. If you throw the dice m times, you will move m x n squares round the edge, i.e. right round the board n times. Out of these m throws, you will pass GO n times and not pass GO m-n times and these will be mixed as evenly as possible.

The main part of **DRAW** is concerned with imitating this process. It uses an extra number on the stack, between 1 and m, to represent the position on the board. It loops round m times for m throws, and each time adds n to this position number. If the answer is more than m then it has passed GO so it subtracts in and does a diagonal step. Otherwise, it does a square step.

81

2. Experiment with **DRAW** using the different plotting modes. This shows a use for plotting mode 2 – it updates the **PLOT** position without affecting any pixels.

Plotting mode 3 is more useful than you'd think, because of the property that if you **PLOT** or **DRAW** the same thing twice over you get back to exactly what you started off with.

For instance, try (after **INVIS CLS**)

> 0  24  1  **PLOT** 63  0  1 **DRAW**

> 32  0  1  **PLOT** 0  45  1 **DRAW**

If you wanted to erase the second line, the natural thing to try is

> 32  0  0  **PLOT** 0  45  0  **DRAW**

but this leaves a hole in the first line.

Now try the same all over again, but using plotting mode 3 throughout. When both lines are present there is a hole where they meet, but that isn't so serious; and when you erase the second line (plotting mode 3 again) the hole is filled in.

3. Clear the screen and try

> 0  0  3 **PLOT** 63  20  3  **DRAW**

and then

> -63  -20  3  **DRAW**

in an attempt to erase the line.

It doesn't work, because the irregularities in the line are not the same when you reverse.

When you erase a line, always go over it in the same direction as you originally drew it.

4. Something that is often useful is a *random number generator,* a word whose result is random like the toss of a coin or the spin of a roulette wheel. In fact it is difficult for a computer to produce truly random numbers, because they always obey their instructions rigidly and predictably. It is easier to produce *pseudo-random* numbers, numbers that follow a rule that, although fixed, is sufficiently complicated to appear random. Here is an example.

> 0 **VARIABLE SEED**

> : **SEEDON**
> ( — next value of SEED)
> **SEED @** 75  **U\*** 75  0 **D+**

```
    OVER OVER U<  -  -
    1-  DUP  SEED  !
;

: RND
    (n —pseudo random no. between 0 and n—1)
    SEEDON U* SWAP DROP
;

: RAND
  ( value for seed — )
  ?DUP 0=
  IF
    15403  @ SWAP
  THEN
     SEED !
;
```

Never mind how these work; you'd better just treat them as recipes.

Each time **SEEDON** is executed, it uses the old value of **SEED** to produce a new value, which it also leaves on the stack. If you use **SEEDON** 65536 times then **SEED** gets back to the value it started with and the whole cycle starts all over again, but the order in which **SEED** takes its 65536 values is complicated enough to look random.

**RND** has one operand, and uses **SEEDON** to produce a pseudo-random number less than this operand. For instance, 6 RND produces a result between 0 and 5, and 6 **RND 1+** produces a result between 1 and 6 — what you'd use for computerized dice.

**RAND** you could probably do without most of the time. It sets **SEED** with the value from the top of the stack, so that you know how the sequence of random numbers will start off. This is useful for debugging, because it means you can have the same pseudo-random numbers each time you test your program. An extra facility in my **RAND** here is that if you say 0 **RAND**, **SEED** is initialized using a system variable that says how many television frames have been displayed (50 each second) since the computer was switched on. This is more truly random.

5. Try this, using **RND** and so on from Exercise 4.

```
:  MEASLES
   ( plotting mode — plotting mode)
   CLS
   BEGIN
      64 RND 46 RND
      3 PICK PLOT 0
   UNTIL
;
```

# Chapter 14

## SAVING PROGRAMS ON TAPE

As you know, when you turn the Ace off it forgets everything except what was built into it in the factory. However, this doesn't mean that you have to leave it on all the time, because you can save your own programs on a cassette tape.

For this, you need an ordinary cassette tape recorder connected to the Ace as described in Chapter 3.

You will also need a cassette tape. There are some advantages in using a short one (for instance you don't have to search so far to find your program), but it's not vitally important. Cheap quality tape will probably work, but if you have trouble you might get better results with a better tape.

Now type in your favourite words, e.g.

> **: FLATTER-ME**
> **CR .** " I sincerely belive you're the"
> **CR .** " most wonderful human being I've"
> **CR .** " ever met.  You're really"
> **;**

To save this on tape, type in

**SAVE** CREEP

but don't press ENTER yet. **SAVE** is the word that does the saving; and CREEP is the name that will identify the program when it's on tape. You don't have to specify that you're saving **FLATTER-ME,** because **SAVE** just saves the entire portion of the dictionary that was defined by you (rather than being built-in to the computer). CREEP does not refer to a defined FORTH word: it's just a label that you choose.

Now wind the tape to a place where, first, you know it's proper tape and not just plastic leader at the beginning, and, second, if there was anything recorded there before, you don't mind erasing it. Start it recording, and then press ENTER. After about 5 seconds you will hear two quick bursts of sound through the loudspeaker, and OK will come up. The sound was the way the computer coded the dictionary so that it could record it on tape.

Now as far as the computer is concerned, it's saved the dictionary, but you must always make sure that it completed its journey to the tape: you do this with a word **VERIFY.**

Wind the tape back to just before where you saved the dictionary, turn the tone control (if there is one) right down and turn the volume up to about three quarters maximum. Type in

**VERIFY** CREEP

(and ENTER) and start the tape playing back. When the tape reaches your saved dictionary, you should see a message saying 'Dict: CREEP' and, about 3 seconds later, OK. If this happens, then well done! If not, you can stop it by pressing the space key.

*What to do if it doesn't work.*
1. Carry out all the checks mentioned in Chapter 3 for when you have trouble loading.
2. Listen to the recording by playing it back through the tape recorder's own loudspeaker (you'll have to unplug the lead from the earphone socket on the tape recorder). You should hear first, a high-pitched whine like a mosquito for 5 seconds; second, a short (less than a second) burst of sound evocative of lazy summer Sundays near Heathrow; third, more of the high-pitched whine (less than a second this time); and fourth, back to Heathrow for about a second.

The mosquito is a leader to let the tape recorder get used to the volume level, and the Heathrow sound is the actual information – first a header saying that it's a dictionary called CREEP, and various other snippets of information, and then the dictionary itself.

These should all be unpleasantly loud if you turn the volume right up. If you can't hear anything at all then for some reason the signal simply hasn't got through to the tape recorder. One possibility is that the plugs on the leads to the computer don't fit quite properly into the tape recorder sockets. Try pulling them out just a fraction of an inch to see if they settle down into a more natural position, and then try saving again.

If the noises sounded all right then try verifying again with the volume turned right up. If the volume's too quiet then the computer won't pick up the signal properly, while if the volume is too loud the signal may get distorted (of the two, this is less likely). If you can't get it to work after trying three or four different volume settings, try saving again.

If you still can't get it to work, you're not having a very lucky day. Vent any surplus aggression on the cat and go to bed. Tomorrow you can buy a much better tape, which is bound to work, and maybe either clean the tape heads on the recorder or borrow a different tape recorder from a friend.

Once you've saved the program and verified it, you can load it back by following the instructions in Chapter 3 – this is really pretty much like verifying.

Remember that when you load a dictionary in from tape, it doesn't erase the dictionary that's already in the computer; it just gets added on at the end. This means that you can store small packages of words separately on tape and load in only those that you happen to need. If you try to load in too much, you get ERROR 10, meaning 'tape error'. There are a few other loading faults that can give ERROR 10 – see Appendix B for more information.

**SAVE, VERIFY** and **LOAD** are used for dictionaries stored on tape. You can also save information more crudely by saying how many bytes you want to save, and what the memory address is of the first one. Instead of **SAVE, VERIFY** and **LOAD,** you use **BSAVE, BVERIFY** and **BLOAD.**

For instance, suppose you want to save a copy of the television picture. This has 768 bytes starting at address 8192, so you use

8192 768 **BSAVE** TVPIC

Again, TVPIC is just a name to go on tape. The mechanical operations with **BSAVE,** when to turn the tape recorder on and off, and so on, are the same as with **SAVE.**

This particular case is one of the rare occasions when you wouldn't verify immediately after saving. The verifying itself changes the screen (by printing up 'Bytes: TVPIC' when it finds the file on tape), so the screen will no longer be the same as it was when you changed it.

To load back TVPIC, the obvious thing to say is

8192 768 **BLOAD** TVPIC

and this will in fact work. However, since you are already loading back TVPIC to exactly the same place as it was saved from, you could also use

0 0 **BLOAD** TVPIC

The rules here are:

1. The first number (i.e. the number that **BLOAD** finds second from the top of the stack) is the address in memory where you want to start loading back to. It doesn't have to be the same as the address where the file was saved from, but if it is you can use 0 instead.

2. The second number (i.e. the number that **BLOAD** finds at the top of the stack) is just a safety precaution. If you forget how many bytes were saved in TVPIC, then it could be dangerous to load it back in — you might find it overwriting memory you wanted to keep. This second number specifies the maximum number of bytes you are prepared to have overwritten. If the file turns out to be bigger than that, then it won't be loaded at all and you'll get ERROR 10.

If you specify 0 for this number, then it means you don't care how big the file is (or you know that it's safe); you want it loaded anyway.

Both these rules apply to **BVERIFY** as well as to **BLOAD.**

Remember that dictionary files and bytes files are quite different, and that the Ace tells you this when it's reading the tape by writing either 'Dict:' or 'Bytes:9' in front of the name. You can't use **LOAD** to load back a bytes file, nor **BLOAD** to load back a dictionary file.

**Summary**

Tape files — dictionary files and bytes files

FORTH words: **SAVE, VERIFY, LOAD, BSAVE, BVERIFY, BLOAD**

**Exercises**

**1.** Having saved the bytes file TVPIC (from address 8192), try

> 9216 0 **BLOAD** TVPIC

to load it back at address 9216. It will change the television picture more or less as before.

So where is the television picture really? At 8192 or 9216? The answer is both. These are, as it were, front door and back door addresses for the same memory boxes.

The front door addresses are 8192 to 9215. When you knock here the computer serves you immediately, even if it means neglecting the television picture (this would show up as momentary white dots). You can't make the tape wait, so the front door addresses are the ones to use when saving or loading the television picture. (Although in practice the tape goes slowly enough for it not to matter much.)

The back door addresses are 9216 to 10239. Here you don't always get immediate service, because the computer may be busy on the television picture. This ensures that if you read or write using the back door addresses, you don't get any white dots.

The character set memory, where all the dot patterns are stored, has a similar system. The front door addresses are 10240 to 11263, and the back door addresses (which we used in Chapter 12) are 11264 to 12287.

**2.** One useful bytes file to save is the character set memory, so that you can load your redesigned characters straight in from tape. Unfortunately, as we mentioned in Chapter 12, you can't read this memory, so you can't save it directly.

The only way round this is to set up somewhere else in memory (the television screen area will do) the bytes that are needed for the redesigned characters. You can then save the bytes from this other area, and later load them back into the character set memory.

**3.** Here's some cunning trickery. Type in your favourite word **(FLATTER-ME)** and then type, all in one bufferful,

> 8896 32 **BSAVE** FLATTER **LOAD** CREEP **FLATTER-ME**

Have the tape recorder recording when you press ENTER, so that you save a bytes file FLATTER. 8896 is the address of the input buffer when it is two lines long, so you are saving the top line of it.

When the noise stops then you have saved the bytes file **FLATTER** and the computer is looking for a dictionary file called CREEP, just after it. Press space to BREAK, and save the dictionary with

> **SAVE** CREEP

Now you have a bytes file FLATTER, which stores one line of the input buffer saying **'LOAD** CREEP **FLATTER-ME'**, followed by a dictionary file CREEP. Load back FLATTER, with

8928 0 **BLOAD** FLATTER

(Note that the address has changed, because the input buffer is now only one line long.)

The computer will load FLATTER into the input buffer, and then, of its own accord, load the dictionary CREEP and execute **FLATTER-ME.**

# Chapter 15

## FRACTIONS AND DECIMAL POINTS

All the numbers you have used so far in FORTH have been *integers (i.e. whole numbers)* and in many versions of FORTH you aren't allowed any other sort. In fact it is surprising how far you can get with integers alone, but just for convenience the Ace also allows you to use decimal fractions. Numbers like this are called *floating point* numbers (although the reasons for this are rather technical).

Here is an example of some floating point arithmetic:

2.1   2.1 **F+ F.**

(The decimal point here is just a full stop.)

There is a most important rule to remember here: you must always tell the computer that it is dealing with floating point numbers and not integers. To do this, you must use the floating point words **F+** and **F.** instead of + and .. (Just for comparison, try

2.1   2.1 **+ .**

to see what happens. The answer, 16673, doesn't really mean anything.)

There are also floating point versions of —, *, / and **NEGATE,** and they are all formed with an F in front: **F—, F*, F/** and **FNEGATE.** They are all written after their operands in the usual FORTH way.

*All* floating point numbers in Ace FORTH are written with decimal points, and this applies even to integers when floating point arithmetic is to be done on them. Suppose, for instance, you want to divide 11 by 4 to get the correct answer of 2.75 instead of the integer answer, 2. You must use the floating point division, **F/,** and so the numbers 11 and 4 must also be made floating point by having decimal points in them:

11. 4. **F/ F.**

There is an extra possibility when writing floating point numbers, which is that you can use what is often called *scientific notation.* Immediately after a floating point number (with a decimal point as usual) you can write E and an integer. This integer is called an *exponent,* and indicates that the floating point number is multiplied by 10 the number of times shown by the exponent. For instance,

```
2.1E0=2.1
2.1E1=2.1 *10=21.
2.1E2=2.1 *10*10=210.
2.1E3=2.1 *10*10*10=2100.
```

If the exponent is negative then the floating point number is instead divided by 10:

```
2.1E-1=2.1/10=.21
2.1E-2=2.1/10/10=.021
2.1E-3=2.1/10/10/10=.0021
```

Another way of looking at the exponent is to imagine it shifting the decimal point along some number of places.

There are two more words associated with floating point numbers, and they are used for converting between floating point and integers.

**INT** converts from floating point to integer, dropping anything after the decimal point. For instance,

```
    12.99 INT .
  - 12.99 INT .
```

gives 12 and -12.

**UFLOAT** converts from integer to floating point, so that

```
    12 UFLOAT F.
```

gives 12. A quirk with **UFLOAT** is the way it works with negative numbers: it adds on 65536 before floating them. (This will make more sense after Chapter 17.) As a consequence of this, the result is never negative. This explains the 'U' in **UFLOAT** (it stands for 'unsigned').

---

Note -- There are limits on the size of floating point numbers that the computer can handle. Considering just positive numbers for the moment, they must lie between 1.0E-64 and 9.99999E62. If you go outside this range, the calculations might look all right, but they are liable to give the wrong answer. Similarly, negative numbers must lie between -9.99999E62 and -1.0E-64.
**INT** will only give the right answer if it is in the normal range for integers, i.e. -32768 to 32767.

---

If you want to rearrange floating point operands on the stack, you need to remember that each floating point number takes up the space of *two* integers. For instance, to drop a floating point number from the stack, you need to do an ordinary, integer, **DROP** twice.

You may like to define your own floating point stack rearrangement words. Here are some definitions of the common ones.

```
: 2DROP
  ( f.p. no. — )
  DROP DROP
;

: 2DUP
    ( f.p. no. — f.p.no., f.p. no.)
    OVER OVER
  ;

: 2SWAP
    ( fp1,fp2 — fp2,fp1)
    4 ROLL 4 ROLL
;

: 2OVER
  ( fp1,fp2 — fp1,fp2,fp1)
  4  PICK 4 PICK
;

: 2ROT
    ( fp1,fp2,fp3 -- fp2,fp3,fp1)
    6 ROLL 6 ROLL
;

: 2@
    ( address — fp)
    DUP @ SWAP 2+ @
;

: 2!
    ( fp, address —)
    ROT OVER ! 2+ !
;
```

## Summary

Floating point numbers
FORTH words: **F+, F-, F\*, F/, FNEGATE, INT, UFLOAT**

## Exercises

1. Define **2ROLL** and **2PICK**, floating point versions of **ROLL** and **PICK**.

2. Which of these are sensible?

> 2 3 F/ F.
> 2 7.6 F+ F.
> 2 2.5 F*
> 2 3 + .

(Answer — none of them. Work out what they ought to be.)

3. The techniques of floating point arithmetic fill many big books, so I'll just show you an example or two.

Square roots: The square of a number is the number multiplied by itself; taking a square root is the reverse process. You want to find the number whose square is some given number. For instance, 16 is the square of 4, so 4 is the square root of 16. Usually you can't calculate square roots exactly, because the answer is an infinite decimal. The square root of 2, for instance, is approximately 1.41421.

This word **SQRT** calculates the square root of a floating point number.

> : **SQRT**
> ( floating point no. — square root)
> 1. 10 0
> **DO**
>     2OVER 2OVER F/ F+        •
>     .5 F*
> **LOOP**
> **2SWAP 2DROP**
> ;

This uses what is called the *Newton-Raphson* method. You start off with a very rough approximation (1.) to the square root, and then each time round **DO LOOP** refines it to a better approximation.

What happens if you do -2. **SQRT ?** Every square is positive, so in fact -2. can't possibly have a square root. Nonetheless, **SQRT** still tries giving a nonsense answer.

4. Here is a word to calculate the sine of an angle, expressed in radians. It is accurate to three decimal places for angles around $2\pi$, and five decimal places for angles around $\pi$ or less. It sums the terms in the power series

$$\sin x = x - \frac{x^3}{3*2} + \frac{x^5}{5*4*3*2} - \frac{x^7}{7*6*5*4*3*2} + \cdots$$

> : **SIN**
>     (x – sine of x)
>     **2DUP 2DUP 2DUP F* FNEGATE**
>     **2ROT 2ROT** ( –x*x, x, x)
>     27 2

```
    DO
        ( --x*x, sum so far term in power series)
        6 PICK 6 PICK ( copy — x*x to top)
        F* | | 1+ *
        UFLOAT F/ ( --x*x, sum next term)
        2DUP 2ROT F+ 2SWAP ( —x*x, next sum, next term)
        2
    +LOOP
    2DROP 2SWAP 2DROP
    ;
```

Here are words for the cosine and tangent.

```
    :   COS
        (x — cosx)
        1.57080
        2SWAP F- ( pi/2 - x)
        SIN
    ;


    :   TAN
        ( x - tan x)
        2DUP SIN
        2SWAP COS F/
    ;
```

# Chapter 16

## READING THE KEYBOARD

From what you've seen so far, the only control you have over how a word executes is through the stack: you can type in the operands before the word itself. Here now are some ways in which the word can get information either direct from the keyboard or from what you type in after the word.

The easiest way is with a word **INKEY** that simply reads the keyboard. If you are pressing a key (it takes the shifts into account too) then **INKEY** leaves its ASCII code on the stack; otherwise, or if you're pressing several keys, it leaves 0 on the stack. ( — ASCII code).

There are many different ways of using **INKEY.** If you have a program to play a fast game, then you might want to move something on the screen if the player is pressing 5, 6, 7 or 8 (the keys with arrows), and otherwise leave it where it is to be shot at. If your program is more relaxed you might simply want to wait for the user to press any key, as with this word **WAIT:**

```
: WAIT
   (—)
   BEGIN
     INKEY
   UNTIL
;
```

Or you might want to wait for the user to press a key, and leave its ASCII code on the stack:

```
: KEY
( — ASCII value)
   BEGIN
     INKEY ?DUP
   UNTIL
;
```

Here is a more elaborate word. It prints "(Y/N)?" and waits for the user to press 'y' or 'n'.

It leaves 1 on the stack for 'y', 0 for 'n'.

```
: Y/N
   ( — 0 or 1)
```

```
." (Y/N)?"
BEGIN
 INKEY DUP ASCII y =
 IF
   DROP 2
 ELSE
   ASCII n =
 THEN
 ?DUP
 UNTIL
 1-
;
```

**INKEY** reads straight from the keyboard, so it is only good for reading one character at a time. There are also a number of words that play with the input buffer, thus giving the program a chance to deal with entire words that you type in.

First, there are two words that stop the program and allow you to type anything you like into the input buffer, using the cursor movements and so on in the usual way if you need to. When you press ENTER the program continues, presumably to analyse your typing.

**QUERY** clears out the input buffer first, and then lets you type.

**RETYPE** doesn't clear out the input buffer, so you have a chance to edit what was there. The cursor is initially ▧, meaning, 'Do you want to change any of this?'.

Neither of these affects the stack in any way.

Next, there are four words to deal with the input buffer once you have typed into it.

The simplest is **LINE,** which just interprets the input buffer as numbers and FORTH words in the usual way. It even gives you ▧ for an unrecognised word, so it acts exactly like the usual process of interpreting a line. However, when it has finished the line, it continues with your program. Its effect on the stack depends entirely on what happens to be in the input buffer.

Here is a word **INPUT** that provides a very simple means of letting a program stop to allow you to type in a number. (If you know BASIC you've probably been waiting for this.)

```
: INPUT
  ( — ?)
  QUERY LINE
;
```

This is extremely flexible, because it allows you to do calculations to produce your number - for instance if the number you want to type in is 32*23 but you can't be bothered to multiply this out yourself, for **INPUT** you can just type in

```
32  23  *
```

However, it also puts a lot of trust in the users, because they can easily type in something that leaves more than one number on the stack, and that would probably lead your program astray.

Here is a modified version of **INPUT** that, while not foolproof, provides a pretty good measure of protection. It plants -32768 on the stack and checks that it is still there afterwards.

```
:   INPUT
    ( - ? )
    -32768 QUERY INVIS LINE VIS SWAP -32768 -
    IF
        ." Hello, hello, hello, what's"
        CR ." going on here, then?"
        QUIT
    THEN
;
```

We use **INVIS** and **VIS** here because normally **LINE** copies the input buffer to the upper part of the screen in the usual way (although it doesn't print OK). You'd probably want to suppress this when a program is running.

Note the word **QUIT** here when an error is found. **QUIT** jumps out of the entire program not only **INPUT,** but all the words currently being executed and lands you back in the usual command state where you type in numbers and words to be executed. Note that the **QUERY LINE** in **INPUT** manages to imitate this command state, but **QUIT** bypasses this and goes right back to the true command state. **QUIT** doesn't clear the stack. There is a word **ABORT** that is much the same as **QUIT**, except that it does clear the stack.

You can get more control over the input buffer by analysing it word by word: there are three words to do this, namely **NUMBER, FIND** and **WORD-** Each, it it finds what it is looking for, will take it from the beginning of the input buffer and (unless invisible mode has been set with **INVIS**) copy it up to the upper part of the screen.

**NUMBER** seeks a number (integer or floating point) at the start of the input buffer. If there isn't one, it simply leaves 0 on the stack. If there is, **NUMBER** copies it up to the upper part of the screen, and leaves its value on the stack together with (on top) a code number to distinguish between integers (code number=4102) and floating point numbers (code=4181).

Here is an example, a word **INTEGER** to get an integer from the input buffer. If the input buffer does not start with an integer, then a retype is offered.

```
:   INTEGER
    ( — integer)
    BEGIN
        RETYPE NUMBER DUP 4181 =
        IF
        ( floating point number)
        ." ignored "
```

96

```
        DROP DROP DROP 0
        THEN
        UNTIL
    ;
```

The next word, **FIND,** is used for finding words that are defined in the dictionary. Each word definition occupies some space in memory, and has an address (technically known as the *compilation* address) to show whereabouts in memory the definition is. When **FIND** finds a defined word at the start of the input buffer, it copies it up and leaves its compilation address on the stack. For instance, type in

> **FIND DUP .**

and it will print the compilation address of **DUP.**

Notice the way things are taken out of the input buffer one at a time and copied up:

1. The Ace is looking for words to execute, and the first one is **FIND.** It copies it up, and at this point the input buffer contains

> **DUP .**

2. Now the Ace executes **FIND**. It again looks for a word, this time so that it can leave the compilation address on the stack. It finds **DUP** and copies it up, leaving just

> .

in the input buffer.

3. Having executed **FIND,** the Ace starts looking for another word to execute. It finds . , copies it up (leaving an empty input buffer) and executes it, printing the compilation address of **DUP.**

4. Having executed . the Ace starts looking for another word to execute. There are none, because the input buffer is empty, so it stops, prints OK, and waits for you to type more.

Note how each word is taken out of the buffer when it is used. Even in invisible mode this happens, although they are not then copied up to the top.

A word that makes use of compilation addresses is **EXECUTE** (compilation address —). It takes a compilation address off the stack and executes the corresponding word. Bear in mind that if you use **REDEFINE** some of the compilation addresses may change.

The next word is **WORD,** which is useful even for nonsense words that are neither numbers nor defined in the dictionary. Knowing that spaces are never part of a word but are used to separate words off from each other, it locates the first word in the input buffer. It copies the word to the top of the screen as usual, but also copies it to the beginning of an area of workspace known as the *pad,* first clearing the pad out with spaces. The pad consists of 254 bytes of RAM memory, starting at address 9985, and is used as an area of workspace for dealing with text. The word **PAD** puts its starting address, 9985, on the stack.

97

Let us look more closely at what **WORD** does.

First, it clears the pad out with spaces.

Second, it takes an operand off the stack, which is the ASCII code for the *delimiter* to be used. Although we said that spaces were used to separate words, which means that the space character is the delimiter, this role could be played by any other character. Whether you use a space or some other character, you must leave its ASCII code on the stack for **WORD**. Remember that the space has ASCII code 32; for other characters you'd use **ASCII.**

Third, **WORD** locates a word at the start of the input buffer. It ignores delimiters before the word, and reads it up to either a delimiter or the end of the buffer.

Fourth, it takes the word out of the input buffer and copies it to the top of the screen (if in visible model and to the pad, starting at address 9986. This copying includes the delimiter (or a 0 if the word was at the end of the line). It puts the length of the word (not including the delimiter) into the very first byte of the pad, at address 9985.

Fifth, it stacks the address 9985 of the pad.

Suppose for example you type in

32 **WORD** axolotl .

Naturally you haven't defined a word **AXOLOTL,** but **WORD** doesn't care about that. 9985 will be printed out by ..

The first few bytes of pad are now.

| Address | | |
|---------|------|------------------------|
| 9985 | 7 | length of 'axolotl' |
| 9986 | 97 | ASCII code for a |
| 9987 | 120 | ASCII code for x |
| 9988 | 111 | ASCII code for o |
| 9989 | 108 | ASCII code for l |
| 9990 | 111 | ASCII code for o |
| 9991 | 116 | ASCII code for t |
| 9992 | 108 | ASCII code for l |
| 9993 | 32 | ASCII code for space |

You can check this for yourself with **C@** and ..

Also try

9986 7 **TYPE**

to see the word `axolotl` printed out.

When text is stored in memory, we need to know where it is and how long it is. We have here two ways of specifying this.

1 **TYPE** uses the address and length explicitly, and takes them from the stack.

2. When **WORD** sets up the text (in the pad) it precedes it with a byte containing the length. All it needs to leave on the stack is the address.

Many versions of FORTH have a word **COUNT** that converts the address of method 2 into the address and length of method 1 : (address address+1, length). Here is how to define it for yourself.

```
: COUNT
    DUP 1+ SWAP C@
;
```

Here is an example that uses **WORD** and COUNT. It takes a message that you type in, and moves it across the middle of the screen over and over again.

```
: MESSAGE
    ( — )
    ASCII ~ WORD  CLS
    BEGIN
      32 0
    DO
      10 I AT SPACE DUP
      COUNT TYPE ( Print message one place to right)
      11 0 AT 32 SPACES ( Erase any part that
      spilled over to next line)
      1500 0
      DO
      LOOP
    LOOP
      0
    UNTIL
;
```

We've used `~` (symbol shifted A) as the delimiter for **WORD**, so that you can put spaces in the message, e.g.

MESSAGE Hello there! ~

If you miss out the ~ then the spaces at the end of the input buffer will count as part of the message.

Remember that it doesn't matter whether the input buffer is left over from your original typing (as in the example with **MESSAGE)** or the program stops to let you type more in (as in **INTEGER**): **LINE, NUMBER, FIND** and **WORD** still act on it in the same way.

**Summary**

The pad and the input buffer

Forth words: **INKEY, QUERY, RETYPE, LINE, QUIT, ABORT, NUMBER, FIND, EXECUTE, WORD, PAD**

**Exercises**

1. Many versions of FORTH contain a word **—TRAILING (** address, length with spaces — address, length without spaces) that starts off with the address and length of some text (as produced by **COUNT** and used by **TYPE)** and changes the length to exclude any spaces at the end of the text. Write a definition of **—TRAILING**. Make sure it works if the text is all spaces.

2. Define a word

```
: PCT
    PAD COUNT TYPE
;
```

You can easily use **PCT** to see what's at the start of the pad. Investigate what the following words do to the pad: **ASCII, SAVE, LOAD, :** . They all have some effect on it, so text stored there by **WORD** is not safe forever.. also uses the pad, but at the other end.

3. Since the pad is only 255 bytes long, there is a limit to how long a word **WORD** can pick up. **WORD** will take at most 253 characters from the input buffer; if there are any left over in the word then the byte at the start of the pad will show 254 (even though only 253 characters have been taken). Try this out, using 32 **WORD** and long strings of characters.

4. Some time when the computer is empty, define

```
: FOREVER
    BEGIN
    QUERY 0
    UNTIL
;
```

This is very difficult to BREAK, because you need to press ENTER to get out of **QUERY**, and then press BREAK before it gets back into **QUERY** again. You can sometimes do it by keeping SHIFT down and pressing ENTER and SPACE almost simultaneously, but it's not easy. The best cure is not to write a word like **FOREVER**.

# Chapter 17

## OTHER WAYS OF COUNTING

In English, as in most languages, counting proceeds in blocks of ten: after a bit of initial wavering, it settles down as

> twenty, twenty-one, ... , twenty-nine
>
> thirty, thirty-one, ... , thirty-nine

and so on.

This grouping into tens is reflected even more rigidly in the usual way of writing numbers, with ten digits 0, 1, 2, 3, 4, 5, 6, 7, 8 and 9.

Mathematically speaking, ten is nothing special as a number and we use it simply because humans have ten fingers each .-. in fact *digit* really just means *finger*. Penguins would never dream of counting in tens, because they have two flippers instead of ten fingers. They count in *twos*.

How do they make this work? First, instead of our ten digits 0 to 9, they have just two penguin digits, 0 and 1. They also call them *bits* instead of digits. When a penguin starts counting it manages 0 and 1 all right, but then gets stuck because there are no more bits for it to use. We would go on to 2 because we've got eight more digits available to take us up to 9, but then we get stuck in the same way.

Our answer is to start using pairs of digits instead of single ones: after 9 comes 10, meaning one ten and no units. The penguin answer is exactly the same, except that they have to start using it much earlier: having run out of bits with one, they write two as 10, and three as 11. Then they get stuck again, so they apply the same process a further stage and write four as 100.

| Number | Human | Penguin bits |
|--------|-------|--------------|
| Nought | 0 | 0 |
| One | 1 | 1 |
| Two | 2 | 10 |
| Three | 3 | 11 |
| Four | 4 | 100 |
| Five | 5 | 101 |
| Six | 6 | 110 |
| Seven | / | 111 |
| Eight | 8 | 1000 |
| Nine | 9 | 1001 |
| Ten | 10 | 1010 |
| Eleven | 11 | 1011 |
| Twelve | 12 | 1100 |

| Thirteen | 13 | 1101 |
| Fourteen | 14 | 1110 |
| Fifteen | 15 | 1111 |
| Sixteen | 16 | 10000 |

If you want to pretend to be a penguin, type

## 2 **BASE C!**

so that you can add 10 and 10 to get 100:

## 10 10 **+** .

**BASE** is a variable provided by the computer itself, *a system variable*. However, unlike ordinary variables its value is just one byte and you must use **C@** and **C!** with it instead of @ and !. Its value is the *number base you* are currently using, or how many fingers the computer thinks you have. Having set **BASE** to two, you must type integers in using the penguin notation. (Floating point numbers are different – they are always in base ten except for the exponent part which uses **BASE**.) The computer will also print the numbers out in penguin.

To get back to human notation, type

## 1010 **BASE C!**

because 1010 is penguin for ten. A useful word here, which would have done the same, is **DECIMAL: DECIMAL** sets **BASE** to ten. *Decimal* here means 'based on tens', as in 'decimal coinage', so our notation is a decimal system. The penguin notation, based on twos, is a *binary* system.

The Jupiter Ace is designed for use by many different species, not just humans and penguins, and you can set **BASE** accordingly. A three-toed sloth, counting on one foot while it hangs on to a branch with the other three, would set **BASE** to three; a fork would set **BASE** to four; and a one-armed bandit would set **BASE** to five.

Animals with more than ten fingers have a different sort of problem when they reach ten. Although they've used up our decimal digits, they need some more of their own before they can get on to their 10. The rule is to start using letters, like the sixteen-fingered typist from the moon Ganymede that we employ at Jupiter headquarters. She starts off with our digits 0 to 9, and then uses the letters A to F for ten to fifteen. Only at sixteen does she need to write 10, and then she carries on to 19 (twenty-five), 1A (twenty-six), then to 1F (thirty-one), 20 (thirty-two) and so on.

This system, with base sixteen, is called *hexadecimal* or *hex* for short.

To summarise then, you need as many digits as you have fingers. If you have more than ten then you'll need not only our usual ten decimal digits, but a few letters as well.

The importance of this lies in the fact that most computers are just like penguins. They store numbers using electrical voltages that can have one of two levels (low=0, high=1), or electronic switches that can be either off (0) or on (1), so they use the penguins' binary system.

This is why powers of two crop up so often with the Ace. A byte, for instance, is a number between 0 and 255, and this is precisely the kind of number that can be written down with just eight bits:

the smallest byte is nought=00000000 in binary.

the biggest is two hundred and fifty-five=11111111 in binary.

---

How do we work out what a binary number means? In decimal notation the different columns represent different values:

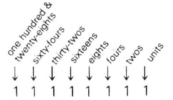

2 5 5

so 255 means two hundreds + five tens + five units.

In binary the same principle applies, except that the columns represent powers of two instead of powers of ten:

1 1 1 1 1 1 1 1

Thus in binary, 11111111 means

| | Decimal |
|---|---|
| one * one hundred and twenty-eight | 128 |
| + one * sixty-four | 64 |
| + one * thirty-two | 32 |
| + one * sixteen | 16 |
| + one * eight | 8 |
| I one * four | 4 |
| + one * two | 2 |
| + one * one | 1 |
| = two hundred and fifty five | 255 |

A quicker way is to imagine adding 1 to it, which will give the binary number 1 0000 0000. The 1 is in the two hundred and fifty-sixes column, so 11111111 is one less than two hundred and fifty-six.

---

An ordinary integer on the Ace is coded into two bytes or sixteen bits, so on the face of it you'd think integers ranged from 0 to binary 1111 1111 1111 1111 (which is
65535 in decimal – you might remember this as the largest possible address in memory). However, we also need a way of storing negative numbers, so for this we use the rule:

A negative number is stored in the computer with 65536 added to it.

Suppose then our integers are between -32768 and 32767, which is what we said before. 0 and the positive numbers, 1 to 32767, are stored just as they are. The negative numbers -32768 to -1 are stored as the numbers 32768 to 65535, so they start where the positive numbers leave off and carry on up to the largest possible number that can be stored in two bytes.

This method of storing negative numbers is known as *twos complement* form.

From this we see that two bytes stored in the computer can be interpreted in two different ways: either as a *signed* number, between -32768 and 32767, or as an *unsigned* number, between 0 and 65535. Which interpretation we use will often depend on the circumstances.

For instance, you have already seen . which prints out a number. There is also a word **U.** (standing for 'unsigned dot') which prints out the same number, but interpreted as an unsigned number. If you type in -1 then it is stored as -1 +65536=65535 on the stack, but you don't usually notice this, because . decodes it back into the negative number -1. **U.**, however, prints out 65535. This means that different words can interpret the same number in different ways. Try also typing in 65535 and printing it out using . .

Another word that works on unsigned integers is **U<** ( integer, integer    flag).     This is just like < except for using unsigned integers – try

> 1   -1 < .

and

> 1   -1 **U<** .

**U<** treats -1 as 65535, which is greater than 1.

Finally, here is useful shorthand for writing binary numbers: take a number written in binary and separate the bits into groups of 4, starting at the right-hand end. If the leftmost group has less than four bits, then put some 0s in front of it. Next, replace these groups by digits and letters according to this table:

| Group of bits | Replace by |
|---|---|
| 0000 | 0 |
| 0001 | 1 |
| 0010 | 2 |
| 0011 | 3 |
| 0100 | 4 |

| | |
|---|---|
| 0101 | 5 |
| 0110 | 6 |
| 0111 | 7 |
| 1000 | 8 |
| 1001 | 9 |
| 1010 | A |
| 1011 | B |
| 1100 | C |
| 1101 | D |
| 1110 | E |
| 1111 | F |

For instance, a hundred, which in binary is 110 0100, is replaced by 64.

This handy rule turns out to be exactly the same as writing the number in hex (base 16), and it works because $16=2^4=2*2*2*2$.

Similarly, if you divide the bits into groups of 3 then you end up using *octal* (base 8) and this too is often used with computers.

## Summary

Number bases -- binary, octal, decimal, hex (hexadecimal)
Signed and unsigned numbers
FORTH words: **BASE, DECIMAL, U., U<.**

## Exercises

1. Why is binary useful when you redesign graphics characters?

2. Try

### BASE C@ .

Charge the number base, and try again. Why is the number base always 10 however much you change it?
Write a word **.BASE** that prints out the number base in decimal. Make sure the number base is the same after **.BASE** as it was before.

3.    Set the number base to 36. Then the digits to use are the ten decimal digits and the twenty-six letters. Any undefined word with three letters or digits gets stored as a number, so you can say things like

### CAT DOG . .

4.    The rule for negating an integer was to subtract it from 65536. In binary, there is a very easy way of doing this: subtract from 65535 and then add 1. This is easy because in binary 65535 is all 1s and subtracting another number from that is the same as changing 0s to 1s and 1s to 0s (1-0=1, 1-1=0)

105

This first step is called taking the *ones complement;* when you have done the second step of adding 1, you have taken the *twos complement.*

5. If you use hex a lot, define a word

    **: HEX**
      16 **BASE C!**
    **;**

6. Work out $2^{10}$ (the answer is 1024). Because this is so close to 1000, it is often used as a kind of binary equivalent of 1000 and is called a K. K here stands for *Kilo,* because it is a bigger version of the small k in kilometre or kilogram.
  It is very useful for working out approximately how big powers of two are. For instance,

$$2^{11} = 2*2^{10} = 2K = \text{about 2000 (actually 2048)}$$
$$2^{20} = 2^{10} *2^{10} = \text{about a million (actually 1048576)}$$

# Chapter 18

## BOOLEAN OPERATIONS

In Chapter 9 we saw how **IF** interpreted numbers as *conditions*, being either *false* (zero) or *true* (non-zero). There are some operations – **AND**, **OR** and **XOR** – that combine conditions, although you need to make sure that the conditions are proper flags, either 0 or 1. These are called *Boolean* operations, after the mathematician George Boole.

Suppose within a word definition you have two conditions, and you want to do something or other if they are both true – i.e. if the first condition is true *and* the second condition is true. You would use **AND** for this. For instance, the top of the stack is between 10 and 20 if it is greater than 9 *and* less than 21. You would first get the results of these two conditions on top of the stack by

**DUP** 9 > **SWAP** 21 <

Now the stack has two flags on top. **AND** will replace them by 1 if they are both 1, i.e. if the top is 1 and the second from the top is 1. Otherwise **AND** will replace them by 0. After **AND**, you can use **IF** and whatever it is you wanted to do.

We can describe this action of **AND** with a *truth* table in which, given the two operands, we can look up the result.

|                   |   | Top of stack | |
|-------------------|---|:---:|:---:|
|                   |   | 0 | 1 |
| Second from top   | 0 | 0 | 0 |
|                   | 1 | 0 | 1 |

You use **OR** when you want to perform your action if either the first condition is true or the second is true (*or* implicitly, if both are true). Note that this last part, that if both conditions are true so is the result of **OR**, is not always the way English works. Suppose you also own one of the *JOKER* computers made by our rivals Saturn of Cambridge Ltd, and it breaks down. When you send it back, they offer you either the same computer (unmended) or a cheaper one in exchange; but if you say,. 'Fair enough, I'll take both', they're more likely to fill your mouth in with concrete.

Here is the truth table for **OR**.

|  |  | Top of stack | |
|---|---|---|---|
|  |  | 0 | 1 |
| Second from top | 0 | 0 | 1 |
|  | 1 | 1 | 1 |

The last Boolean operation is **XOR**, which stands for 'exclusive **OR**'. This is like **OR**, except that it doesn't contain the 'or both' part. In other words, for its result to be true, one of the operands must be true but not both. Here is its truth table.

|  |  | Top of stack | |
|---|---|---|---|
|  |  | 0 | 1 |
| Second from top | 0 | 0 | 1 |
|  | 1 | 1 | 0 |

We said that **AND**, **OR** and **XOR** only work properly with true and false numbers if the true numbers are definitely 1 (and not some other non-zero value). What happens then if the numbers on the stack take other values?

Let's take **AND** first. We know how **AND** works on 0 and 1, so this tells us how **AND** could work on bits, *bits* being just 0 or 1. Therefore with arbitrary numbers we can write them as rows of bits (by using binary notation) and **AND** together corresponding bits to get corresponding bits in the result.

For instance, suppose the top of the stake is 106 (binary 110 1010) and the second from the top is 201 (binary 1100 1001). Our **AND** calculation is then

```
      0000 0000 0110 1010
      ↕↕↕↕ ↕↕↕↕ ↕↕↕↕ ↕↕↕↕
AND   0000 0000 1100 1001
      0000 0000 0100 1000
```

so the result is binary 100 1000, or 72. **OR** and **XOR** work bit by bit in exactly the same way.

Here is a rather typical example that shows **AND** being used in two quite different ways. Let us define a word **LETTER?** that tests an ASCII code to see if it represents a letter, putting 1 on the stack if it does and 0 if it doesn't.

The capital letters have ASCII codes between 65 and 90, and the lower case letters have codes between 97 and 122 so here is one version (making use of **ASCII**).

```
: LETTER?
    ( ASCII code — flag)
    DUP ASCII A 1- >
    OVER ASCII Z 1+ < AND
    SWAP DUP ASCII a 1- >
    SWAP ASCII z 1+ < AND OR
;
```

108

However, there is a very slick trick that is typical of the way one can play with ASCII codes. Each lower case letter has an ASCII code that is exactly 32 more than the code for the corresponding capital. If you write the codes in binary, you discover that to change from lower case to upper case, you just change one of the bits from 1 to 0, e.g.

> A has code in binary 0100 0001
> a has code in binary 0110 0001
>                           ↑
>                    change this bit

We can do this with **AND**: we just **AND** the ASCII code with binary 1101 1111 (decimal 223) which leaves seven bits unaltered, but changes the crucial bit to 0.

This leads to a short cut in **LETTER?**: we can first convert to upper case and then check that the code lies between 65 and 90.

> : **LETTER?**
> ( ASCII code — flag)
> 223 **AND**
> DUP ASCII A 1- >
> SWAP ASCII Z 1+ < AND
> ;

## Summary
FORTH words: **AND, OR, XOR**

## Exercises
1. We stressed that to use **AND, OR** and **XOR** on true/false conditions, they must be 0 or 1. Actually, this is only the case for **AND** and **XOR**; for **OR** a true condition can be anything non-zero. Why is this?

2. Define a word **&** that takes two numbers off the stack and leaves 1 if they are both true in the non-zero sense, and 0 if one of them is false. (Use **IF ... ELSE ... THEN**.) Define words corresponding to **OR** and **XOR** in the same way as **&** corresponds to **AND**.

3. You can think of the 223 in **LETTER?** as a mask that tells **AND** to leave certain bits of the other operand (the ASCII code) unchanged, and to force a certain bit to 0.

Similarly, a mask can tell **OR** to leave certain bits unchanged and to force the rest to 1; and a mask can tell **XOR** to leave certain bits unchanged and to switch the rest over, whatever they were originally.

Work all this out in detail.

-1 **XOR** takes the top of the stack and *complements* all its bits, changing 0s to 1s and 1s to 0s. How does this work? (Hint: what is -1 in binary?) This is the ones complement of chapter 17, exercise 4.

# Chapter 19

## MORE ADVANCED ARITHMETIC

We have seen already that with one byte you can store 256 (=$2^8$) possible numbers, and with two bytes you can store 256*256=65536 possible numbers (0 to 65535 unsigned, or -32768 to 32767 signed). With four bytes, you could store $256^4$=4294967295 possible numbers, so if you had a pair of ordinary two-byte numbers you could handle much bigger numbers.

This is the principle behind *double length* arithmetic. Some words assume that the two top numbers on the stack are not separate numbers, but the two halves of a double length 4-byte number. These words are not as comprehensive as the words for single length (2-byte) arithmetic. They aim at providing the minimum facilities you need to define whatever extra double length arithmetic you need.

**D+** ( d1, d2 — d1 +d2) adds together two double length integers (which we've written here as d1 and d2) on top of the stack.

Here's a silly example silly, because you could do it much more easily with single length arithmetic. It adds 3 to 5.

$$3 \quad 0 \quad 5 \quad 0 \text{ } \textbf{D+} \text{ } ..$$

First, to get a double length integer on the stack you must put on two single length integers: 3 and 0 for a double length version of 3; 5 and 0 for 5. If you write 3 out in eight hexadecimal digits, it is

$$0000 \mid 0003$$
$$\uparrow \mid \uparrow$$

| more significant half higher up on stack | less significant half lower down on stack |

Hexadecimal is useful here, because the two single length numbers you need to work out for the stack correspond exactly to the first four hex digits (the *more significant* part, which goes higher up on the stack) and the last four hex digits (the *less significant* part, which goes lower down on the stack). If you have an integer written in hex (4C83A2, say) and you want to put it on the stack as a double length integer, then first make sure it has exactly eight hex digits. If if has more than eight then give up, but our case has fewer so you can put 0s in front to give 004C 83A2. To put this on the stack, set **BASE** to 16 and type

$$83A2 \quad 004C$$

In other words the hex digits are the same, but you type the second group of four *first*.

Note -- if your number is negative, then put any extra 0s in front before you take the twos complement. The twos complement uses the same method as in Chapter 17, Exercise 4: take the ones complement by changing binary 0s to 1 s and 1s to 0s or subtracting from hex FFFFFFFF, and then add 1.

If your numbers are really single length but you need to do double length arithmetic on them then you won't need to consider hex notation. To get the double length version on the stack,

1. Put the single length number on the stack.
2. Put either 0 or -1 on the stack. Use 0 if the number is 0, or positive or unsigned, use -1 if the number is negative.

Here are some more words for double length arithmetic.

**D<** ( d1, d2 — flag). 1 (true) if d1 is less than d2.

**DNEGATE** ( d — -d) negates the double length integer d.

**U\*** ( n1, n2 — n1 \*n2) does a multiplication. The two numbers n1 and n2 on the stack are *unsigned single length* integers. The result, their product, is also unsigned, but it is *double length*. Remember that not only are the numbers here treated as being unsigned (as suggested by the U in the name), but the answer is also double length.

        256    256 **U\*** . .

gives 1 and 0, the two parts of the double length number 65536  (hex 10000).

**U/MOD** ( d1 , n2 remainder d1/n2, quotient). As suggested by the U in the name, this a version of **/MOD** in which all the numbers involved are treated as being unsigned. As in **U\***, there is some double length arithmetic involved as well: the dividend d1 (the number you divide into) is double length. All the other numbers are single length

**\*/** ( n1, n2, n3  — (n1 \* n2)/n3) You have seen this before, in Chapter 5. I can now explain that while **\*/** is calculating it works out n1 \* n2 as a double length number. This preserves accuracy, even though 'you never see any double length numbers on the stack, **\*/MOD** is similar.

We now go on to see some ways of controlling how a number gets printed out, i.e. of *formatting* the number. This is defined to work on double length integers. However, you will also find it useful on single length integers so remember the rules above for putting 0 or -1 on the stack to convert single length to double length.

The problem with outputting numbers is that the best way is to calculate the digits in the wrong order To; output 123  you can easily work out the 3 -. divide 123  by 10, giving 12   remainder 3, this remainder is the last digit. When we repeat the process, dividing 12 by 10, we get the next to last digit, 2; and finally we get the first digit 1. This method works with any number base.

FORTH provides a method of storing these digits backwards in the pad until they are all there.

**<#** starts this off.

**#>** finishes it by dropping a double length integer from the stack and leaving the address of the first digit and the number of digits (ready for **TYPE**).

In between you use **#** and **#S** to produce the digits.

**#** ( d1 — d2) produces one digit out of an unsigned double length integer on the stack. It divides it by the current number base (in **BASE**), leaves the (double length) quotient on the stack, and uses the remainder to put a digit in the pad.

**#S** ( d1 0 — 0,0) is **#** repeated until the double length integer on the stack is 0. In other words, it produces all the digits. Note that if the original double length integer d1 is 0, then **#S** produces one 0 digit.

All that **#** and **#S** can store in the pad are the digits, but you can also put in any other character you like using **HOLD**

**HOLD** ( ASCII code —) stores a character (with the given ASCII code) in the pad in the same way as **#** stores a digit.

Here is a word **MONEY** to print out a sum of money that is stored on the stack as the number of pence, a single length integer.

```
: MONEY
    ( pence -)
    0 ( make double length)
    <# # # ( two digits for pence)
    ASCII .   HOLD ( decimal point)
    #S ( pounds)
    ASCII £ HOLD #> TYPE
;
```

Note how everything goes backwards between **<#** and **#>**.

Here is another example, which shows that you can do calculations within **<#** . . . **#>** but you must be careful to remember whether you've got single- or double-length Integers) It takes a time in seconds, and prints it as hours minutes seconds

```
: MINSEC
    ( divides top of stack by 60 and stores in pad two digits
  from remainder followed by a colon)
    ( n — n/60)
    60   /MOD SWAP
    0 # # DROP DROP
    ASCII : HOLD
;

  : TIME
    ( no. seconds —)
    <# MINSEC ( :seconds)
    MINSEC ( :minutes)
    0 #S ( hours)
    #> TYPE
  ;
```

The last word connected with **<#** and **#>** is **SIGN** ( integer —). **SIGN** takes a single length signed integer off the stack and, if it is negative, **HOLD**s a minus sign. Remember that **#** uses unsigned numbers, so if you want to print signed numbers you must apply **#** to the absolute value, and use **SIGN** at some point. Here, for instance, is a word **D.** to print a signed double length integer.

```
: D- >PAD
  ( double length integer —)
  DUP >R DUP 0<
  IF
    DNEGATE
  THEN
    <# #S R> SIGN #>
;

: D.
  ( double length integer —)
  D->PAD TYPE
;
```

Note that the sign of a double length integer is shown by the 32nd (most significant) of its 32 bits (1 for negative, 0 for positive or zero), and this is the same as the sign of the single length integer that forms the more significant part (2 bytes) of the double length integer. In **D- >PAD**, we start off with the two parts of the double length integer on the stack:

( less significant part, more significant part)

**DUP >R** stores the more significant part on the return stack to remember the sign.

We still have the signed double length number on top of the stack, and our next step is to negate it (with **DNEGATE)** if it is negative. Then we can use **#S** to hold the digits of the absolute value, and **R> SIGN** to hold the sign.

You can now see double length arithmetic working more clearly — try things like

256 256 **U\* D.**

Here are some definitions of double length versions of single length arithmetic words. How do they work?

```
: D0=
   ( d — flag)
   OR 0=
;

: D0<
   ( d — flag)
   SWAP DROP 0<
;

: DABS
   ( d — absolute value of d)
   DUP 0<
   IF
      DNEGATE
   THEN
;
```

Try writing more of your own. You can use **2DROP** and so on from Chapter 15 for double length integers.

A sort of opposite of formatted output is **CONVERT**, which converts text into a double length integer. The general idea can be shown by seeing how the characters "123" can be converted into a number, using base 10. We use an *accumulator,* initially zero, to store the number we have read up to: at each stage we multiply the accumulator by 10 and add on the next digit. We shall write the accumulator in English just to make clear the distinction between the text "123" and the number (actually stored in binary) in the accumulator.

First stage: accumulator=nought.

Second stage: read the "1". Multiply the accumulator by ten and add one, giving one.

Third stage: read the "2". The accumulator becomes one\* ten + two = twelve.

Fourth stage: read the "3". The accumulator becomes a hundred and twenty-three.

This is really just the reverse of **#S**. You can see that you can replace "ten" by any other number base.

**CONVERT** starts off with a double length accumulator on the stack — probably nought, but maybe you've accumulated an earlier part of the number already. On top

114

of the accumulator is the address of the character *one byte before* the text you want to read. **CONVERT** reads the characters of the text one by one, adjusting the accumulator, until it finds one that isn't a digit (in the current number base). It then stops, leaving on the stack the new accumulator and the address of this non-digit,

(accumulator, address of byte before text
− new accumulator, address of non-digit)

As an example, here is a word **CONVERT,** that reads in a double length integer starting at a given address, ignoring commas,

: CONVERT,
( address − double length integer, address of terminator)
1− 0  0 ROT
BEGIN
    CONVERT DUP C@ ASCII , −
UNTIL
;

Finally in this rather mixed chapter I shall describe how floating point numbers are set up. Like a double length integer, a floating point number uses four bytes, but in a quite different way. Any floating point number can be written in the form

.xxxxxxEy

in scientific notation, with a decimal point, 6 decimal digits xxxxxx (the first one not 0), and an exponent part y. Thus 123.456 would be written .123456E3, and .0001234 would be written .123400E-3.

The Ace uses three of the four bytes in a floating point number to store the six digits. since four bits can store a number between 0 and 15 *(a hex* digit), they can easily store a decimal digit, so a byte can store two decimal digits, one in each of the groups of four bits. (This is known as *binary coded decimal,* because the number is not converted fully into binary: only its decimal digits are.)

You can see this by changing the number base to 16, and typing

123.456 **U.  U.**

43|12   3456

exponent  binary coded decimal
byte    digits

Note that when 123.456 is on the stack, it occupies two ordinary stack entries. The one lower down contains the last four binary coded decimal digits (3456), and the one higher up contains the first two digits (12) and the exponent byte. The possible exponents range from - 63 to 63, so they can be stored as binary in seven bits. For technical reasons, they are not stored by the usual method for storing signed integers; they are made positive by having 64 added to them. This *offset* exponent then lies in the range 1 to 127 and can be stored in seven bits.

There is one remaining bit in the exponent byte, and that shows the sign of the entire floating point number: 1 for negative, 0 for positive. This is in the same place as the bit that shows the sign of a double length integer, so you can use **D0<** for floating point numbers too (i.e. as an **F0<** ).

The floating point number 0. is special. All four of its bytes are zero. This means you can also use **D0=** for floating point numbers (as an **F0=**).

## Summary

Double length integers
Formatted output
Floating point numbers
FORTH words: **D+**, **D<**, **DNEGATE**, **U\***, **U/MOD**, **\*/**, **<#**, **#**, **#S**, **#>**, **HOLD**, **SIGN**, **CONVERT**

## Exercises

1. Write a version of **MONEY** that always prints three digits for the number of pounds, using * characters on the left if the number of pounds itself hasn't got enough digits (e.g. print £89.95 as £*89.95).

2. Try defining these double length versions of words you know already: **D-**, **D=**, **DMAX**, **DMIN** and **DU<**.

Another word available in some implementations of FORTH is **D.R.**

**D.R** ( d, n —). Here d is a double length integer to be printed and n is the number of characters it is to print (with spaces used on the left to fill up any unused room). Here is a definition of **D.R**, using the **D->PAD** we defined for **D.**.

```
: D.R
 ( d, n — )
 >R D->PAD
 R> OVER - SPACES TYPE
 ;
```

Note that if the number is too big to fit in the n places, then it runs over at the end.

Define a word **S->D** to convert a signed single length integer to a double length one.

# Chapter 20

## INSIDE THE DICTIONARY

As you know, when a word is defined, its definition is put in the dictionary. So far you've seen three different kinds of words, defined by :, **CONSTANT** and **VARIABLE**, and although these three may seem very different, in fact there are certain general principles that apply to all words.

1. Every word has a name.

2. Every word contains some information specifying *(a link* to) the previously defined word. This means that all the words are linked together in a long chain, each one saying where the next one is. The chain starts at the newest word and works its way (in the order you see in **VLIST**) to the oldest, which has a code showing that it is linked to nothing.

3. Every word has some information (a 2 byte code called the *code field)* showing generally what is to be done when the word is executed: e.g. stack a number (for **CONSTANT**), start executing some more FORTH words (for :).

4. Almost every word has some more information (its *parameters)* that is like the code field but more specific: e.g. the number to be stacked (for **CONSTANT**), or the FORTH words to be executed (for :).

The name, link and code field have the same format for every conceivable kind of word, so these are grouped together into the *header* of the word. Every word has a header.

The parameters are very variable in format; they could be anything from a single number to a long FORTH program. How they are used depends on the code field. They are called the *parameter field.*

These principles are quite general, and mean that FORTH words are not restricted to those defined by :, **CONSTANT** and **VARIABLE**. The simplest way of making your own sort of word is with **CREATE**. **CREATE** makes a word with a header but no parameter field, and puts it in the dictionary.

You may imagine that its lack of parameter field makes it quite useless, but this is not so for the following reasons. First, you can (and probably will) make up your own parameter field for it, and second, the code field specifies that when this new word is executed it leaves on the stack the address of its parameter field and does nothing else. You can then pick up this address to use the parameter field in your own way.

One common way of using **CREATE** is to make super-variables that can store more than one number. (These are called *arrays.)* For instance, you might want to store twelve numbers that are the numbers of days in the twelve months in an ordinary year. You can set up a word **MONTHS** whose parameter field contains these twelve numbers in order:

| Header for **MONTHS** | 31,28,31,30,31,30,31,31,30,31 30,31 |
|---|---|

$$\underbrace{\qquad\qquad\qquad\qquad\qquad\qquad\qquad}$$

parameter field

To set up the header and put it in the dictionary you type in

### CREATE MONTHS

The next problem is to set up the parameter field, and for this you use a word ,.
, (n —) takes a number off the stack and *encloses* it in the dictionary— i.e. it sets aside two extra bytes for the dictionary, and writes the number in.

For the twelve numbers, you'd type

```
31 , 28 , 31 , 30 , 31 , 30 ,
31 , 31 , 30 , 31 , 30 , 31 ,
```

Remember that , is actually a FORTH word, not just punctuation in a list, so you need spaces to separate it from the numbers. Also remember the , right at the end, which is just as necessary as the others.

The word **MONTHS** is now fully defined. To use it, define a word **MONTH** to convert a month (1 for January up to 12 for December) to a number of days.

```
: MONTH
    ( month — no. days)
    1- DUP + MONTHS +
    @
;
```

The definition of **MONTH** will be entered in the dictionary immediately after the final 31 in **MONTHS**.

**MONTHS** leaves on the stack the address of its parameter field, i.e. the address of the 31 for January. We want to add on to this 0 for January, 2 for February, 4 for March, and so on up to 22 for December (the numbers are doubled up because there are two bytes for each month length in **MONTHS**). **1- DUP +** converts from the month code we're given (1 to 12) to the doubled-up month code (0 to 22). When we've added this to the parameter field address of MONTHS, we get the address of the month length we want and @ gets the month length itself.

Here is a similar application, to store the three-letter abbreviations (TLAs) for the days of the week: Mon, Tue, Wed etc. We shall set up a word **DAYTLAS** that contains the 21 characters necessary, and since a character only takes up one byte, we shall use **C,**, a one byte version of , .

**C,** (number — ) encloses a number in the dictionary, like ,, but it only uses one byte of dictionary space instead of two.

118

Typing in **ASCII M C, ASCII o C,** etc could be a bit of a bore, so we define an auxiliary word **STRING,** just to help us define **DAYTLAS.** It takes a word from the input buffer, and encloses its characters in the dictionary.

```
: STRING,
    32 WORD COUNT ( COUNT as in Chapter 16)
    OVER + SWAP
    DO
      I C@ C,
    LOOP
  ;
```

Now type

    **CREATE DAYTLAS STRING,** MonTueWedThuFriSatSun

If you're not going to need **STRING,** again, then a cunning trick you can play is to say

    **REDEFINE STRING,**

which erases **STRING,** and replaces it with **DAYTLAS.**

Now you need a word **.DAY** that, given the number of a day in the week (1 for Monday up to 7 for Sunday), prints out its TLA.

```
: .DAY
  ( day —)
  1-  3 * DAYTLAS +
  3 TYPE
  ;
```

Another word used in setting up parameter fields is **ALLOT** (no. bytes —). This sets aside a number of bytes (specified by the top of the stack) in the dictionary for your parameter field, in the same way as **C,** and **,** set aside one and two bytes; but unlike **C,** and **,** it doesn't store any numbers in these bytes. It just makes the space available as part of the parameter field.

Now for something clever. **CREATE** is rather simple minded in what it does. It only sets up a header, so it doesn't give you any help in setting up the parameter field, and when the new word is executed all the help it gives is to leave its parameter field address on the stack. This is all very well if your word is just a one-off job, but if you have more rather similar words you'll get bored with having to do the same work more than once.

Suppose you want the equivalent of **.DAY** in several languages: **.JOUR** for French, **.TAG** for German and so on. For each one you need

    1. The data (the actual TLAs) including a way of setting it up (this is what **STRING,** does), and

2. A method of using the data to print out the relevant TLA. This is going to be largely the same as **.DAY**.

The only thing that varies from one language to another is the data, so we are going to define a word **MAKEDAYS** that contains both the method for setting up the data and the method of using it. We shall then define **.DAY** by saying

<blockquote>MAKEDAYS .DAY  MonTueWed . . . .</blockquote>

which will use **MAKEDAYS'** knowledge of how to set up data. Now **.DAY** itself contains the data – we don't need a separate **DAYTLAS**. When we use **.DAY** (in the same way as before), it will refer back to **MAKEDAYS** to find out how to use the day number.

Here is how we do it. First, we define **MAKEDAYS**, not with :, but with two words **DEFINER** and **DOES>**. These are always used together. **(FORGET DAYTLAS and .DAY.)**

```
DEFINER MAKEDAYS
  32 WORD 1+ DUP 21 + SWAP
  DO
    I C@ C,
  LOOP
DOES>
  SWAP 1- 3  * +
  3 TYPE
;
```

(Note the ;, just as in a colon definition.)

This is in two parts. The first part, the *defining* part, goes up as far as **DOES>**. When we say

<blockquote>MAKEDAYS .DAY   MonTueWedThuFriSatSun</blockquote>

the first thing that **MAKEDAYS** does is to make a header for **.DAY**, just as **CREATE** does – except that the code field is different, as we shall see. **MAKEDAYS** then executes its defining part, to set up the parameter field for **.DAY** – in our case it reads a string from the input buffer, and encloses twenty-one characters from it in the dictionary much as **STRING,** did. Now **.DAY** is fully defined, and **MAKEDAYS** is finished with for the time being.

The next part of **MAKEDAYS**, from **DOES>** to ;, is the *action* part. It is used when we say something like

<blockquote>3 .DAY</blockquote>

If **.DAY** had been set up by **CREATE**, then not much would happen – **.DAY** would just leave its parameter field address on the stack. However, it can do more than that because it has **MAKEDAYS** to refer back to: **.DAY** still leaves its parameter field address on the stack (on top of the 3 that you typed), but it then goes through the action part of **MAKEDAYS**. This uses the two numbers to print out the relevant TLA.

Type in

> **MAKEDAYS .JOUR** lunmarmerjeuvensamdim
> **MAKEDAYS .TAG** MonDieMitDonFreSamSon
> 4 **.JOUR**
> 5 **.TAG**

This is one of the cleverest ideas in FORTH, so it's well worth mastering. Remember that **MAKEDAYS** is not just any old common or garden word; it has the power to define new words and so is on a par with :, **CONSTANT, VARIABLE** and **CREATE**: it is a *defining* word. **DEFINER**, of course, is even further up in the clouds, because it defines new defining words. In the next chapter, we shall see how it can be used to provide facilities that FORTH in its bare form lacks.

Note: If you are using a defining word (like **MAKEDAYS)** that was defined by **DEFINER,** and while it is defining a new word (like **.DAY)** an ERROR crops up, then the incomplete definition will be left in the dictionary. This won't do any damage, but it is untidy and wastes space, so you should **FORGET** it. There is a way round this explained in Chapter 24, Exercise 5.

Another note — **DEFINER** is done differently on other versions of FORTH. Instead of writing

> **DEFINER** name

you'd write or

> : name **CREATE**

or

> : name **<BUILDS**

The effect is the same, but these other forms are not possible on the Ace: you use **DEFINER** instead.

Finally, here in detail is the format of the header of a word.

First is the name of the word, the *name field.* This has one byte for each character of the name (at most 63). Letters are converted to upper case, and the last character is shown as such by having 128 added to it (i.e. its most significant bit is changed from 0 to 1). This would normally show that the character is inverse video, but not in this case.

Second are two bytes, the *length field,* that store the total length in bytes of the word definition, excluding the name field: 7 for the rest of the header + the length of the parameter field. The length field is filled in when the next word is defined.

Third are two bytes for the *link field,* which is the address of the name length field of the last word defined before the present one.

Fourth is one byte for the *name length field,* the number of characters in the name. This can have 64 added on to make the word an *immediate* word (see chapter 23).

Fifth are two bytes for the *code field,* which specify how the word is to behave.

When you use **FIND**, its result is the code field address of the word found, i.e. the address of its code field. The parameter field follows immediately after the header, so the parameter field address is always 2 more than the code field address.

## Summary
Headers of words – name fields, length fields, link fields, name length fields, code
 fields, parameter fields.
FORTH words – **CREATE, ,, C,, ALLOT, DEFINER, DOES>**

## Exercises
1. If you didn't already have **VARIABLE** and **CONSTANT,** how could you define them with **DEFINER?** Define similar words **2VARIABLE** and **2CONSTANT**that store 4-byte numbers – i.e. either floating point numbers or double length integers.
2. Define a word – **HEAD,** say – with **CREATE,** and compare

> **HEAD .**

with

> **FIND HEAD .**

The first one gives the parameter field address, which is 2 more than the code field address given by the second.
3. Many versions of FORTH have a word ' (pronounced 'tick') which is just like **FIND** except that it gives the parameter field address instead of the code field address. ' is easy to define on the Ace:

> **: '**
>  **FIND 2+**
>  **;**

4. In Chapter 11, Exercise 1, we promised a quicker way of calculating pitch numbers, given semitones. The problem was, given a number $n$ of semitones between 0 and 11, to multiply a fixed bass pitch number by $\left(\frac{1}{2}\right)^{n/12}$, and there we multiplied it by $\left(\frac{1}{2}\right)^{1/12}$ $n$ times. A better way is to store the twelve numbers in an array. We store each one as a fraction, with two numbers (like $17843/18904$ for $\left(\frac{1}{2}\right)^{1/12}$). Define

```
CREATE SCALE 1 , 1 , 17843 , 18904 ,
26547 , 29798 , 16585 , 19723 ,
4813 , 6064 , 5089 , 6793 ,
19601 , 27720 , 6793 , 10178 ,
3032 , 4813 , 5377 , 9043 ,
14899 , 26547 , 9452 , 17843 ,
```

(24 numbers altogether).
The new version of **SEMS** is now

```
: SEMS
  ( semitones above middle C — pitch number)
  36  + ( semitones above bottom C)
  12   /MOD SWAP ( no. octaves, no. spare semitones)
  3822  SWAP
  DUP + DUP + SCALE +
  DUP @ SWAP 2+ @ */
  SWAP ?DUP
  IF
     ( divide by 2 for each octave)
     0
     DO
        2 /
     LOOP
  THEN
;
```

5. Here is a neat way of testing **.DAY**, **.JOUR** and so on, by using **FIND** and **EXECUTE**.

```
: TEST
  FIND 8 1
  DO
     I OVER EXECUTE SPACE
  LOOP
  DROP
;
```

To test **.DAY**, type in

**TEST .DAY**

# Chapter 21

## STRINGS AND ARRAYS

Here are two very useful examples that use **DEFINER**. Strings are sequences of characters manipulated as single units, while arrays are variables that store more than one number. Many computer languages have strings and arrays built into them. FORTH usually doesn't, but as you will see this doesn't matter because you can define the facilities for yourself — or buy someone's cassette tape to do the same thing.

### Strings

A *string* is just a sequence of characters. It is not the same as a word, because a word has a meaning given to it by its definition in the dictionary. A string has no such meaning. FORTH allows you to print strings by using .", but many computer languages allow you to manipulate them in all sorts of ways, so that you can do as many different things with strings as you can with numbers. I shall show you a few examples here just to set you off.

First, we want to find a way of putting strings on the stack, but it is easiest not to do it directly. Whereas we always know how much space a number takes up — two bytes for a single length integer, four for a double length integer or floating point number — a string could be any length. Therefore we keep the string somewhere else in memory, and put on the stack its address and length. This is exactly the form required by **TYPE**, so we already know how to print a string.

The next step is to find a way of setting up variables that store strings instead of numbers. We shall do this with a defining word **STRING**. Its defining part sets up a parameter field that contains, first, one byte for the length of the string (which must therefore be no more than 255 characters), and then the string itself, read in from the input buffer. The action part of **STRING** will convert the parameter field address into the address and length of the string itself — our usual form for specifying a string on the stack. We use the word **COUNT** from chapter 16.

```
DEFINER STRING
  ASCII " WORD COUNT DUP C,
  OVER + SWAP
  DO
    I C@ C,
  LOOP
DOES>
  COUNT
;
```

You define a string like this, typing it all in one bufferful:

> **STRING FREDSADDRESS** 23, Flightpath Lane, Heathrow, 01-750
> Sorry, I missed that."

The double quote " at the end marks the end of the string, because we used **ASCII " WORD** in **STRING**. This enables you to use spaces in the string.

The simplest thing you can do with your string now you've set it up is print it out:

> **FREDSADDRESS TYPE**

A useful operation on strings is taking sections of them, or *substrings*. This is called *slicing*. To specify a substring, you say whereabouts in the original string it starts and finishes. In FREDSADDRESS, "Flightpath Lane" is a substring, starting at the 5th character (assuming you put a space after the comma) and finishing at the 19th. We shall define a word **SLICE** that enables you to say

> **FREDSADDRESS 5 19 SLICE TYPE**

to get "Flightpath Lane" printed out.

**SLICE** has four operands, namely the address and length of the bigger string, and the start and finish within that of the substring. Its two results are the address and length of the substring. Since this is still the usual format for a string, you can do anything to a substring that you could to the original. You can print it out or even slice it again.

> **: SLICE**
> ( address, length, start, finish — address, length)
> **SWAP 1 MAX 3 PICK MIN 1-**
> ( address, length, finish, start—1)
> **SWAP ROT MIN OVER MAX**
> ( address, start—1, finish)
> **OVER — ROT ROT + SWAP**
> **;**

This definition of SLICE also takes care of the cases when the start is too small, or the finish is too big, or the finish is less than the start.

The next facility we shall describe is for comparing strings. The obvious test is for two strings to be *equal*, i.e. to have the same characters in the same order. A more subtle test is for one string to come before another in an extended alphabetical order, and we use the symbols < and > that are used with numbers to mean 'less than' and 'greater than'. We consider one string to be less than another if it comes first in alphabetical order: thus "animal" is less than "bird", "five" is less than "four".

The rules here for determining alphabetical ordering are slightly different from usual, and rely on ASCII codes. To compare two strings, you compare them character by character looking for a place where they differ, and then compare the different characters. This is the usual process that tells you that "boojum" is less than "book". Since all capital letters have smaller ASCII codes than lower case letters, they are also smaller in the string sense. Thus, unexpectedly, "Zoo" is less than "aviary" and "FORTH" is less than "Forth".

Here are some words to define **$=**, **$<** and **$>** (the string versions of =, < and >).

```
: 0<>
  ( n – flag)
  ( tests for n non-zero)
  0=  0=
;

: +COUNT
  ( used in CHECK)
  4 ROLL 1+ 4 ROLL 1-
;

: CHECK
  ( addr1, length1, addr2, length2 – addr3, length3,
    addr4, length4)
  ( Adjusts the addresses and lengths of two strings to
    miss out any initial characters where they agree)
  BEGIN
    3 PICK 0<> OVER 0<> AND
    5 PICK C@ 4 PICK C@ = AND
  WHILE
    ( while neither string finished, & they still agree)
    +COUNT +COUNT
  REPEAT
;

: <DROP
  ( a, b – b)
  SWAP DROP
;

: $=
  ( a1, l1, a2, l2 – flag)
  CHECK ( now strings equal if both lengths are 0)
  <DROP OR <DROP ( now have dropped addresses
        and ORed together lengths)
  0=
;
```

```
: $<
  ( a1, l1, a2, l2 – flag)
  CHECK ROT ( a3, a4, l4, l3)
  OVER 0<> OVER 0<> AND
  IF
    ( neither string has run out, so compare different characters)
    DROP DROP C@ SWAP C@ >
  ELSE
    ( one string starts off the other)
    > <DROP <DROP
  THEN
;



: $>
  ( a1, l1, a2, l2 – flag)
  4  ROLL 4 ROLL $<
;
```

The crucial word here is **CHECK**, which checks along both strings, character by character, until it finds a place where they differ. Thus **CHECK** applied to "boojum" and "book" ends up with their substrings "jum" and "k".

There are some more ideas about strings in the exercises.

### Arrays

An array is a variable that can store more than one number, like **MONTHS**; these numbers are called the *elements* of the array, so **MONTHS** has twelve elements, namely 31, 28, 31 and so on. To specify a particular element, you use its position within the array, and this number is called the *subscript* (in **MONTHS**, the subscripts are 1 for January, 2 for February, etc.).

Because we defined **MONTHS** with **CREATE,** we had to define **MONTH** as well to turn a subscript into the address of an element. If we had used **DEFINER** to define a word **ARRAY,** we could then have used **ARRAY** to define **MONTHS** and **MONTHS** could have both stored the elements and processed the subscripts. (Exercise: do this.)

A more complicated kind of array uses *two* subscripts for each element: it is called a *two-dimensional* array. You should imagine the elements as being arranged in a rectangular table, with the first subscript specifying the row and the second the column. This would be the natural way of storing something like a chess position. (The computer of course, has to store the table row by row.)

Here are some words to enable you to define two-dimensional arrays. These are only examples, because there are lots of facilities you could build in or leave out (see the exercises). Forget the string words first, to give yourself room.

```
: 2*
    ( n — 2*n)
    DUP +
;

: ROW
    ." Row error "
    CR
;

: COLUMN
    ." Column error "
    CR
;

: MESSAGE
    ." Please FORGET this word "
    CR ABORT
;

: ROW?
    IF
        ROW ABORT
    THEN
;

: COLUMN?
    IF
        COLUMN ABORT
    THEN
;


DEFINER 2—D
    ( no. rows, no. columns —)
    DUP 1— 0<
    IF
        ( no. columns is 0 or less)
        COLUMN MESSAGE
    THEN
    OVER DUP 1— 0<
    IF
        ( no. rows is 0 or less)
        ROW MESSAGE
```

```
THEN
C, DUP C, * 2* ALLOT
DOES>
   ( row, column, address of array — address of element)
   ROT ROT 3 PICK ( addr, row, column, addr)
   C@ 3 PICK DUP 1-
   0< ROW? < ROW? ( error message if row wrong)
   DUP 1- 0< COLUMN?
   3 PICK 1+ C@ DUP
   3 PICK < COLUMN? ( error message if column wrong)
   ROT 1- * + 2* +
;
```

To use **2 - D** you'd say, e.g.

### 8 8 2-D CHESSBOARD

or

### 1 12 2-D MONTHS

and then fill in the elements however you want. You use the elements just like variables, with @ and !. For instance to set the element at row 2, column 5 of **CHESSBOARD** to 1, you'd say

### 1 2 5 CHESSBOARD !

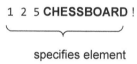

specifies element

specifies element and to get its value back to the stack,

### 2 5 CHESSBOARD @

## Summary
Strings, substrings, string comparison
Arrays, elements, subscripts, dimensions.

## Exercises
1. Here are some more facilities for strings.
(a) Assignation: given two strings on the stack (specified as usual by addresses and lengths), copy the characters from the second one into the first. If the second string is too long, cut it off at the end; if it is too short, pad it out at the end with spaces.

(b) A word to leave just the length of a string (by dropping its address from the stack).

(c) A word to leave the ASCII code of the first character in a string.

2. There are many possibilities for arrays.

(a) When the address of an element is calculated, the subscripts can be checked to make sure they are not too small or too big – as in **2-D**. Alternatively, this checking could be missed out for extra speed.

(b) We specified *upper bounds* for the arrays, i.e. how big the subscripts can be; it was understood that they couldn't be less than 1. It is also possible to specify *lower bounds* to say how small the subscripts can be.

(c) It is possible to have three-dimensional arrays or even worse; the number of dimensions for an array is the number of subscripts needed for each element. More generally, it would be possible for the defining word – no longer **2–D**, but **DIM**, say – to read the number of dimensions off the stack first of all, and put this in the parameter field; then it would start taking the bounds themselves off the stack.

(d) An array could have one byte for each entry instead of two; this would make it useful for storing characters or small numbers. Going in the other direction, an array could have four bytes for each entry, for floating point numbers or double length integers.

(e) The defining word could initialize all the elements to 0 when it defines an array.

(f) An array could be a *constant* array, which gives an element itself rather than its address. The elements would need to be found on the stack when the array is defined.

Some of these are harder to deal with than others. See what you think of them.

3. Two words often found in FORTH, although not in Ace FORTH, are **MOVE** and **CMOVE.** They are quite useful when dealing with strings. Both copy information from one part of memory to another.

**MOVE** (address1, address2, n–) copies the contents of n 2-byte cells starting at address1 into the memory starting at address2.

**CMOVE** (address1, address2, n–) is similar, but copies n bytes instead of n 2-byte cells.

In both **MOVE** and **CMOVE,** if n is 0 or negative then nothing happens. Try writing your own definitions for these.

A problem can arise if the block you are reading from overlaps with the block you are writing to: in this case you must be careful which end of the block you start copying from.

A related word (again not available on the Ace) is **FILL** (address, n, byte –) which fills the memory starting at the given address with n copies of the given byte.

# Chapter 22

## VOCABULARIES

Here is a feature of FORTH that you probably won't use so much. It allows the dictionary to be split up into various *vocabularies,* each with a name (the only vocabulary that exists initially is called **FORTH**). When you choose to use one vocabulary rather than another (by typing in its name), any dictionary search is confined to that vocabulary. This means that you can have two words with the same name, but in different vocabularies so that you can get different interpretations of the word depending on which vocabulary is active.

Suppose you wanted to redefine numbers so that when you type them in, they print out a bingo caller's tag: e.g.

> **: 88**
> **. "** Two fat ladies"
> **;**

This is quite permissible; it means that when you use 88 it is found as a word in the dictionary and prints "Two fat ladies". (Normally for a number, no definition is found in the dictionary and the next step is to try to work it out as a number instead of as a defined word.) However, it is rather dangerous to have these redefined numbers lying around, so **FORGET 88**.

Much safer is to have a separate vocabulary, **BINGO**, to contain them. At the moment, the only vocabulary in the dictionary is **FORTH**, the standard one. To set up **BINGO**, type

**VOCABULARY BINGO**

This does two things:

1. It defines a *vocabulary word* **BINGO**, whose function is to activate the **BINGO** vocabulary. A rather odd feature is that this word **BINGO** is actually in the **FORTH** vocabulary.

2. It sets up a new vocabulary called **BINGO**. So far the vocabulary **BINGO** contains no words of its own (not even the word **BINGO)**, but it does contain all the words of the vocabulary **FORTH**.

**FORTH** is **BINGO**'s *parent,* because **BINGO**'s vocabulary word was set up in the **FORTH** vocabulary. The general rule when searching a vocabulary for some word is that if it is not found the search carries on through the parent vocabulary.

To see this, use **VLIST**. You will see a list of words in the **FORTH** vocabulary, starting with the vocabulary word **BINGO**.

Now type **BINGO**. This makes **BINGO** the *context* vocabulary, i.e. the one in which to look for the words you type in. This is also the vocabulary listed by **VLIST**, so **VLIST** now will list the **BINGO** vocabulary: first the words properly in the **BINGO** vocabulary (there aren't any yet), and then the words in **BINGO**'s parent, **FORTH**. You won't yet see any difference between this **VLIST**, for **BINGO**, and the previous one, for **FORTH**.

Now let's define some words for **BINGO**. **BINGO** is already the context vocabulary (because you typed **BINGO**), but this only affects searches for words. New definitions are entered into the *current* vocabulary, which is still **FORTH**. To make **BINGO** the current vocabulary, use the word **DEFINITIONS**: this makes the current vocabulary the same as the context vocabulary. You must use **DEFINITIONS** to allow yourself to enter new word definitions into the context vocabulary.

By now **BINGO** should be both the context and current vocabularies, so start defining the bingo tags.

```
: 88
  . " Two fat ladies "
;

: 21
  . " Key of the door "
;

: 189
  ." My age "
;
```

Now if you do **VLIST**, you can see the new words **88**, **21** and **189** in the **BINGO** vocabulary. If you do **FORTH** and **VLIST**, you will see only the words in the **FORTH** vocabulary and the numbers 88, 21 and 189 will have regained their proper meanings.

Here more precisely is how vocabularies work. We said in chapter 20 that when a word is defined its header contains a *link* that points to the previously defined word in the dictionary. This is not in fact quite true; the link points to the previously defined word in the current vocabulary, and there may have been words defined in another vocabulary between the two. For instance in our example **189** is linked to **21** which is linked to **88**: this linked chain makes up the **BINGO** vocabulary. **88** is linked to a kind of trick that joins the **BINGO** vocabulary to its parent vocabulary, **FORTH**.

If you did **FORTH DEFINITIONS** to make **FORTH** the current vocabulary, and then defined another word, it would be linked to the word **BINGO** (which, you will remember, is actually in the **FORTH** vocabulary). Thus the vocabularies can be interleaved in the dictionary.

Let us summarize what we've said so far:

1. Initially there is only one vocabulary, **FORTH**.

2. Two of the vocabularies (possibly the same one) are in use at any given time: the context vocabulary is used when looking for words, and the current vocabulary is

used when defining new words.

3. **VOCABULARY** defines a new vocabulary and its associated vocabulary word (but the vocabulary word is contained not in the new vocabulary, but in its *parent*, the current vocabulary).

4. A vocabulary word is used to specify the context vocabulary; **DEFINITIONS** makes the context vocabulary the current vocabulary as well.

5. When the system is searching for a word you have just typed in, it starts off in the context vocabulary, and, if necessary, continues with its parent. It is bound to end up in **FORTH**, because **FORTH** is Adam and Eve as far as vocabularies are concerned.

The parameter field of a vocabulary word is laid out as follows:

First, two bytes containing the address of the name length field of the newest word in the vocabulary. This shows both where to start any search through the vocabulary and where to link the next word to be defined in it.

Next, one byte that always contains 0. This is a kind of fake name length field (no real word has length 0) and works the trick for chaining vocabularies together. If our vocabulary has any children, then their first (oldest) words are linked to this byte.

Finally, two bytes that contain the address (called the *vocabulary linkage*) of the corresponding two bytes in another vocabulary: not the parent vocabulary, but simply the last vocabulary to be defined before this one. This means that all vocabularies can be found by starting at the newest and following through from one to the previous one. You won't usually need to use this. In **FORTH**, these two bytes are 0.

There are three variables associated with vocabularies. The first two are called **CONTEXT** and **CURRENT**, and their values are the addresses of the parameter fields of the vocabulary words for the context and current vocabularies.

The third one hasn't got a name, but its address is 15413. The value of this variable is the address of the two bytes containing the vocabulary linkage in the newest vocabulary. This shows where to start if for some reason you want to check through all the vocabularies.

If you start using vocabularies, you need to be careful with **FORGET** and **LOAD**.

With **FORGET**, the safest rule is: don't forget words from more than one vocabulary at once. If you forget a vocabulary word then the system of vocabulary linkages will no longer be right. (This only matters if you want to use the vocabulary linkages yourself.)

With **LOAD**, again the vocabulary linkages will no longer be right.


## Summary

Vocabularies — context and current.

Vocabulary words, vocabulary linkages.

FORTH words: **FORTH**, **VOCABULARY**, **DEFINITIONS**, **CONTEXT**, **CURRENT**.

# Chapter 23

## INSIDE COLON DEFINITIONS

This chapter explains how to give yourself more control over colon definitions — it also applies to definitions made by **DEFINER** (or, as we shall see, by **COMPILER**).

You must have realised by now that a word from the input buffer is treated differently when you are in the middle of a colon definition: it's not executed immediately, but stored away as part of the definition. We say that normally we are in *interpret mode* (because the words are being interpreted and executed), but that while a word is being defined by a colon definition we are in *compile mode* (the words from the input buffer are compiled into the dictionary as part of the new definition).

Even in a colon definition you can switch back temporarily to interpret mode, using two words [ and ].

[ takes you into interpret mode.

] takes you into compile mode.

(Note that the computer only prints OK in interpret mode. This helps you remember which you're in.)

For instance, suppose you have two numbers in a word definition, and you find it natural to type them in using different number bases. You would use [ and ] to go into interpret mode while you change **BASE**. The word **TAB** in exercise 4 of chapter 12 is a bit like that, because the 31 is more naturally binary 11111. You might well prefer to type it in as

> : **TAB**
> ( tab stop —)
> 15388 **@** -
> [ 2 **BASE C!** ]
> 11111
> [ **DECIMAL** ]
> **AND SPACES**
> ;

(When you've done this, try

> **LIST TAB**

None of the interpret mode stuff will be shown in the listing, and in fact binary 11111 will be converted to decimal 31.)

It should be clear from this that [ is in some way special, because even though the

134

computer is in compile mode when it meets **[**, it executes it rather than compiling it into the dictionary. This is because **[** is what is called an *immediate* word, a word that is always executed immediately even in compile mode.

You can define your own immediate words very easily. You just define them in the usual way, and then execute the word **IMMEDIATE. IMMEDIATE** makes the newest word (actually, the newest word in the current vocabulary) into an immediate word.

If you wanted to write quite a few definitions with both binary and decimal numbers, you could define

```
: BASE2
  2 BASE C!
;

IMMEDIATE

: BASE10
  DECIMAL
;

IMMEDIATE
```

and then

```
: TAB
  ( tab stop -)
  15388 @ -
  BASE2 11111 BASE10
  AND SPACES
;
```

Again, **BASE2** and **BASE10** don't come out in the listing of **TAB.**

One use of **[** and **]** is that you can do calculations while in the middle of defining a word. What is more, by using an immediate word **LITERAL,** the results of these calculations can be compiled into the definition as though you'd typed them straight in as numbers in compile mode.

If you wanted to fill the screen with dots, you could use **CR** and then print 23 * 32 dots. Now 23 * 32 = 736, but maybe you can't be bothered to work this out. Using **LITERAL,** you could define a word **DOTS** thus:

```
: DOTS
  CR
  [ 23 32 * ] LITERAL ( 23 32 *)
  0
  DO
    ." ."
  LOOP
;
```

**LITERAL** (n —) takes a single length integer off the stack, and compiles it into the dictionary in the same way as a number would normally be compiled.

Notice our comment ( 23 32 *). When you list **DOTS** there is no trace of the fact that you used **LITERAL**, so the comment reminds you of what's going on.

We have now seen both ordinary words, which in compile mode are compiled to execute later, and immediate words which are executed immediately. There are quite a few very important words that must do both.

;, for instance, has an immediate effect which is to go back into interpret mode. But it also needs to be compiled into the definition to mark the end when the compiled words are finally executed. We say it has a *compile-time* (or immediate) action ("Don't try to compile any more of this definition") and a *run-time* action ("Don't try to execute any more of this definition").

Similarly, **LITERAL** has both a compile-time action (take a number off the stack and compile it into the definition) and a run-time action (take the number that has been compiled just here and put it on the stack).

**IF**, **THEN**, **BEGIN**, **DO** and the rest have a similar double nature: at compile-time they work out how the word definition is sectioned up by these structures, and at run-time they must make any necessary jumps round the sections. Such words are called *compiling words* because they compile things into the dictionary.

There is a word **COMPILER** that enables you to define your own compiling words, but before I say how it works I shall explain what compiling involves in a bit more detail.

As we know from chapter 20, every FORTH word has what is called a *code field* in its header: so the address of the code field is called the *code field address* of the word. (This is the address that **FIND** leaves on the stack.) When the word is compiled into the definition of another word, all that happens is that its code field address is enclosed in the dictionary (using ,). For this reason, the code field address is often called the *compilation address*.

One word that uses compilation addresses is **EXECUTE** (compilation address —). It takes a compilation address off the stack and executes the corresponding word, e.g.

### FIND DUP EXECUTE

when typed in in execute mode does the same as **DUP**.

A simple colon definition has just a list of compilation addresses in its parameter field. To execute the word, the Ace takes the first of these compilation addresses, finds out the word whose compilation address it is, executes that word, comes back to go on to the next compilation address, and so on. Eventually it reaches the compilation address for [the run-time action of] ;, and then it knows it has finished this word.

For instance, if you define

```
: 2*
   DUP +
;
```

then the definition for 2* has

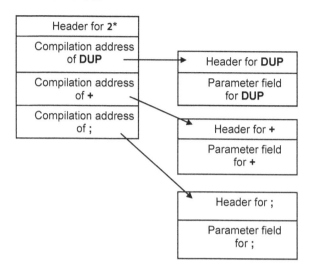

(**DUP**, + and ; are all in ROM, and their parameter fields are rather different.)

This is the simplest form, but quite often there must be some extra information after the compilation address. For instance **LITERAL** compiles a number into the definition, and this number is stored in the dictionary immediately after the compilation address of **LITERAL**. Numbers typed directly into the definition are compiled in the same way.

This extra information is called the *operand field,* and the whole caboodle (compilation address + operand field if there is one) is called a *compiled word.* The compiled word set up by **LITERAL** consists of its compilation address followed by the operand field, two bytes for the number from the stack.

Another example is **IF**. Its operand field has two bytes saying how far to jump to get over the **IF . . . ELSE** section if the condition turns out to be false.

To set up your own compiling word, you need to specify
1.   how to set up the operand field: this is the compile-time action, and
2.   how to execute the compiled word: this is the run-time action.

You specify both of these with two words **COMPILER** and **RUNS>** - like **DEFINER** and **DOES>,** they always occur together.

Here is a word **2LITERAL** that works like **LITERAL** but with four bytes instead of two - so you can use it for floating point numbers or double length integers.

```
4 COMPILER  2LITERAL
   SWAP , ,
RUNS>
   DUP @ SWAP 2+ @
;
```

The compile-time action is to take two entries off the stack and compile them into the dictionary (with ,). This is the part before **RUNS>**.

The run-time action is the part after **RUNS>**. **RUNS>** leaves the address of the operand field on the stack (rather as **DOES>** leaves the address of a parameter field) so that you can fetch the four-byte number stored there.

Notice the 4 before **COMPILER**. This shows how many bytes you intend to put in the operand field. It's up to you to make sure you get it right, because if you don't the computer can get very confused. If the number of bytes might vary, then you use -1 **COMPILER** and your compile-time action must set the first two bytes in the operand field to show the length of the rest of the operand field (excluding these two bytes). ( and ." use this mechanism.

To show how to use **2LITERAL**, suppose you need a word to add 1/7 to a floating point number on the stack. One way is

```
: 1/7+
    1. 7. F/ F+
;
```

However, since 1/7 is 0.142857 the word **1/7+** would run much more quickly if you typed it in as

```
: 1/7+
0.142857 F+
;
```

Now, rather than work out this number beforehand you can type it in as

```
: 1/7+
[ 1. 7. F/ ] ( 1/7)
2LITERAL F+
;
```

At compile time (when **1/7+** is defined) **2LITERAL** will put a compiled word into the definition of **1/7+** : first its own compilation address (or rather a compilation address for its run-time action) and then an operand field containing the floating point number. At run-time (when **1/7+** is executed) it will copy the number from the operand field to the stack.

Be very careful if you edit **1/7+**. The listing mechanism doesn't know what the operand field means, so it just ignores it. **LIST 1/7+** produces

```
: 1/7+
( 1/7)
2LITERAL F+
;
```

and the only record of the floating point number is in the comment. If you edit **1/7+**, you must type the calculation that leads to 1/7 in all over again.

A word that can be useful is **HERE** (— address). This puts on the stack the address where the next byte enclosed in the dictionary will go. It shows how far in memory the dictionary has reached.

## Summary

Compile mode and interpret mode.
Immediate words, compiling words.
Compiled words: compilation address and operand field.
FORTH words: **[, ], IMMEDIATE, EXECUTE, COMPILER, RUNS>, HERE.**

## Exercises

1. One way of using **EXECUTE** is with a compilation address stored in a variable. For instance, you may have two different ways of dealing with unwelcome enquiries:

> : **RUDE**
> **CR ."** Go and boil your head."
> ;
>
> : **POLITE**
> **CR ."** That's very interesting, and my"
> **CR ."** colleague Richard would be"
> **CR ."** pleased to discuss it with you."
> ;

> **FIND POLITE VARIABLE MOOD**

As it stands, **MOOD** contains the compilation address of **POLITE**. But if you wake up with a hangover, or if Richard starts sending the enquirers back to you, you could say

> **FIND RUDE MOOD !**

In either case, to get the appropriate response you use

> **MOOD @ EXECUTE**

This is quite useful, but there is a big drawback if you ever use **REDEFINE**: **REDEFINE** can change the compilation addresses of words, but it wouldn't have any way of knowing that it ought to adjust the values of variables like **MOOD** and you'd have to do this yourself. The compilation addresses that are likely to change are those of the words that are newer than the old version of the word you redefine.

Similarly, **LOAD** can change compilation addresses. If there is already a dictionary in memory when you load a new one in from tape, the new dictionary will have all its compilation addresses changed.

# Chapter 24

## HOW THE MEMORY IS LAID OUT

Various parts of the memory have various uses in the Ace; some have ROM, some have RAM and some aren't used at all. Here we describe the various parts giving their addresses in both hex (first) and decimal (afterwards, in brackets).

0 (0) to 1FFF (8191): this uses ROM and so the information stored there is indelibly built into the computer (unless you take it through one of those X-ray machines at an airport). It contains computer programs to tell the Ace what to do, including all the Ace's own FORTH word definitions.

2000 (8192) to 23FF (9215): this is exactly the same RAM as is at addresses 2400 to 27FF, so each of these RAM bytes has two addresses. Reading or writing has a different effect depending on which address you use. The smaller address gives priority to the FORTH program and the larger address gives priority to the circuitry that produces the television picture. This is explained more fully in Chapter 14, Exercise 1.

2400 (9216) to 26FF (9983): this is the *video* RAM. It stores the television picture, with the ASCII code of each of the 24*32 characters that make it up.

2700 (9984): this is RAM and should always contain the byte 0.

2701 (9985) to 27FF (10239): RAM, storing the pad. (See Chapter 16.)

2800 (10240) to 2BFF (11263): more addresses for the RAM between 2C00 and 2FFF, with the same distinction as for the video RAM.

2000 (11264) to 2FFF (12287): this is the *character set* RAM, containing the dot patterns for 128 characters. See Chapter 12. Note that you can't read back from this RAM: you can only write to it.

3000 (12288) to 3BFF (15359): three identical copies of the RAM 3000 to 3FFF.

3C00 (15360) to 3C3F (15423): this RAM contains the *system variables*. These are various pieces of information that the Ace needs to store, and they're described more fully below.

3C40 (15424) to 3FFF (16383): RAM containing the dictionary, the stack and the return stack.

The dictionary starts at 3C40 with the vocabulary word **FORTH,** and continues with your own words. Where it finishes depends entirely on how many words there are. After the dictionary there are twelve bytes unused (so that stack underflow doesn't corrupt the dictionary) and then the stack, growing upwards through memory.

The return stack starts at 3FFF and grows down in memory, towards the stack. When they get too close there is no more room left and you get ERROR 1.

| Dictionary | 12 Bytes | Stack → | ← Return stack |
|---|---|---|---|
| 3C40 | | | 3CFF |

It is possible to provide more memory for the dictionary and stacks (it is plugged in at the back of the computer), and this will start at address 4000 (16384) and may extend up as far as FFFF (65535). However much you provide, the return stack will start at its top end (the end with the highest address) and work down.

## System variables

Here is a list of system variables. We have given them all names, but that is just for ease of reference. The Ace will not recognize these names, except for a few, like **BASE,** that are FORTH words. I've written these FORTH words in bold type in the usual way.

FP_WS 3C00 (15360) 19 bytes used as work space for floating point arithmetic.

LISTS 3C13 (15379) 5 bytes used as work space by **LIST** and **EDIT.**

RAM 3C18 (15384) 2 bytes — the first address past the last address in RAM. If you want to set aside some RAM at the top end as not being available for the dictionary and stacks, then store its starting address at RAM and do **QUIT. QUIT** clears the return stack and starts it off again at the address stored in RAM.

HOLD 3C1A (15386) 2 bytes. The address of the latest character held in the pad by formatted output (#, **HOLD** and so on).

SCRAPS 3C1C (15388) 2 bytes. The address of the place in the video RAM where the next character is to be printed (i.e. the *print position*). The example **TAB** (Chapter 12, Exercise 4) uses this.

INSCRN 3C1E (15390) 2 bytes. The address of the start of the current *logical line* (what I called before a computer line) in the input buffer.

CURSOR 3C20 (15392) 2 bytes. The address of the cursor in the input buffer.

ENDBUF 3C22 (15394) 2 bytes. The address of the end of the current logical line in the input buffer.

L_HALF 3C24 (15396) 2 bytes. The address of the start of the input buffer. The input buffer itself is stored in the video RAM, where you see it.

KEYCOD 3C26 (15398) 1 byte. The ASCII code of the last key pressed.

KEYCNT 3C27 (15399) 1 byte. Used by the routine that reads the keyboard.

STATIN 3C28 (15400) 1 byte. Used by the routine that reads the keyboard.

EXWRCH 3C29 (15401) 2 bytes. This is normally 0, but it can be changed to allow printing to be sent to some device (e.g. a printer) other than the television screen. EXWRCH must be given the address of a machine code (see the next chapter) routine to output a character. The character is provided in the A register of the Z80. The output routine should preserve the auxiliary registers, ix and iy, and finish off with *exx* and *ret*.

FRAMES 3C2B (15403) 4 bytes. These four bytes form a double length integer that counts the time since the Ace was switched on, in 50ths of a second. It can thus be used as a clock. Here are some words to use it.

```
: SETCLOCK
( hours, minutes —)
BEGIN
   INKEY 0= ( wait for ENTER to be released)
UNTIL
CR . " Press a key to set clock"
SWAP 60 * + ( time in minutes)
3000 U* ( time in 50ths of a second, double length)
BEGIN
   ( wait for key depression)
   INKEY
UNTIL
0 15403 !
15405 ! 15403
;
```

(Exercise 3 explains the rather devious way in which we set the counter.)

```
: MINSEC
( double length seconds or minutes — single length minutes or hours)
( writes seconds or minutes to pad)
60 U/MOD SWAP
0 # # DROP DROP ( write seconds or minutes)
ASCII : HOLD
;
```

```
: TIME
( prints time using formatted output)
15403 @ 15405 @
OVER OVER D+ ( time in 100ths of a second)
<# # # ( print fractions of a second)
ASCII . HOLD ( now double length time in seconds on stack)
MINSEC ( print seconds, leave single length time in minutes)
0 MINSEC ( print minutes, leave single length time in hours)
0 #S #> TYPE
;
```

142

Warning — if these four bytes ever reach hex FFFFFFFF then the next change, to 00000000, will also affect the system variable XCOORD. Also, note that **BEEP** and tape operations temporarily stop the frame counter.

XCOORD 3C2F  (15407) 1 byte. The x-coordinate last used by **PLOT**. **DRAW**, in Chapter 13, exercise 1 uses this to tell it where to start the line.

YCOORD 3C30  (15408) 1 byte. The y-coordinate last used by **PLOT**.

**CURRENT** 3C31  (15409) 2 bytes. The parameter field address for the vocabulary word of the current vocabulary. See Chapter 22.

**CONTEXT** 3C33  (15411) 2 bytes. The parameter field address for the vocabulary word of the context vocabulary. See Chapter 22.

VOCLNK 3C35  (15413) 2 bytes. The address of the fourth byte in the parameter field — the vocabulary linkage — of the vocabulary word of the most recently defined vocabulary. See Chapter 22.

STKBOT 3C37 (15415) 2 bytes. The address of the next byte into which anything will be enclosed in the dictionary, i.e. one byte past the present end of the dictionary. **HERE** is equivalent to 15415 @.

DICT 3C39  (15417) 2 bytes. The address of the length field in the newest word in the dictionary. If that length field is correctly filled in, then DICT may be 0.

SPARE 3C3B (15419) 2 bytes. The address of the first byte past the too of the stack. Note — because of the way @ works, 15419 @ will give the address of the top entry on the stack.
  Here is a word that prints out the entire stack, starting at the bottom, without destroying it.

```
: .S
  15419 @ HERE 12 +
  ( top, bottom)
  OVER OVER —
  IF ( if stack not empty)
     DO
       I @ . 2
     +LOOP
  ELSE
     DROP DROP
  THEN
;
```

143

ERR_NO 3C3D (15421) 1 byte. This is usually 255, meaning "no error". If **ABORT** is used, and ERR_NO is between 0 and 127, then "ERROR" will be printed out, followed by the error number ERR_NO.

FLAGS 3C3E (15422) 1 byte. Shows the state of various parts of the system, each bit showing whether something particular is happening or not. Some of these may be useful.

Bit 2 (the 4s bit in binary), when 1, shows that there is an incomplete definition at the end of the dictionary. If **ABORT** is executed, this definition (its address is inferred from DICT) is taken out of the dictionary.

Bit 3 (the 8s bit), when 1, shows that output is to be fed into the input buffer.

Bit 4 (the 16s bit), when 1, shows that the Ace is in invisible mode.

Bit 6 (the 64s bit), when 1, shows that the Ace is in compile mode.

**BASE** 3C3F (15423) 1 byte. The system number base.

**Exercises**
1. Try this-

```
: SYSVARS
  ( shows system variables continuously)
  CLS
  BEGIN
    0 0 AT 15360 80 TYPE
  0
  UNTIL
;
```

You should easily be able to see FRAMES counting away; the other flashing variable is KEYCNT. Just to the left of KEYCNT is KEYCOD – you can see this work if you press a key. Towards the end is the header for **FORTH**.

Why does it all flash every five seconds? (Hint: consider what happens when the least significant byte of FRAMES reaches 13, the ASCII code for carriage return.)

2. The frames counter FRAMES is not updated exactly every 50th of a second, but every 624/625 50ths of a second. This means that the word **TIME** I have given will gain one second in 625, or approximately 2¼ minutes a day. If you want very accurate timing, you'll need to correct this.

3. Suppose you are reading FRAMES, by

15403 @ 15405 @

and the less significant two bytes turn out to be 65535 (i.e. their maximum). It is possible that in between reading the two parts FRAMES will be updated: the two bytes at 15403 will go down to 0, and the two at 15405 will be increased by 1. The double length integer you have read is therefore 65535 too big (about 20 minutes). This sort of thing can happen even within @, so it's quite pernicious. However, there is a way round: if you want to know the exact time at a given moment, then read FRAMES twice (each time read 15403 first and then 15405) and take the *smaller* of the two answers.

The same sort of problem arises in **SETCLOCK.** We first set the two bytes at 15403 to 0, so that we know these can't interfere with the values we are writing in by inconveniently going from 65535 to 0.

4. How long does FRAMES have to count for before it reaches hex FFFFFFFF?

5. In Chapter 20 I said that if you have used **DEFINER** to make a new defining word of your own, and if your word runs into an ERROR while it is half-way through defining another word, then this half-defined word won't be erased from the dictionary. This is why in Chapter 21 we needed the word **MESSAGE** in case this happened while you were defining a new array.

Bit 2 in FLAGS lets you force the partial definition to be erased when **ABORT** is executed: you'd use

> : **MESSAGE**
> ( Sets bit 2 of FLAGS to 1 and aborts)
> 15422 **C@** 4 **OR** 15422 **C! ABORT**
> ;

# Chapter 25

## MACHINE CODE

You will think of the Ace just as a computer that understands FORTH, but that isn't the whole story. At the heart of the Ace is a relatively simple-minded but very hard-working component called *a processor chip* (or, often, *CPU* which stands for Central Processor Unit). It has to read the keyboard, interpret your typing, execute your FORTH programs and display the results, even though by itself it knows nothing at all about FORTH. It has to be told everything by instructions stored in ROM.

The instructions (of course) can't be written in FORTH, and in fact they are written in *machine code* which is the only form the processor understands. In machine code, each instruction is coded into bytes — usually one, sometimes more. When the processor is first switched on, it wakes up and thinks, 'Where was I? I've forgotten. I'd better start at the beginning.' So it fetches a byte from the beginning of memory (address 0) and obeys it as a machine code instruction. After that it goes on to the next instruction and obeys them one after another in sequence; or, if the instructions tell it to, it'll start obeying them from somewhere else in memory. Some of these instructions tell it how to execute FORTH programs.

There are many different kinds of processor, each with its own variety of machine code. The one in the Ace is a Z80 (actually a Z80A, which works faster), a processor originally designed by Zilog Corporation and now used on many different computers.

Explaining Z80 machine code could easily fill another book the size of this one, so I'm not going to try. If you don't already know about it but you want to learn, find yourself a small book whose title and blurb say something to the effect of 'Z80 machine code (or *assembly language)* for the beginner.' In the meantime, you can read the rest of this chapter but you mustn't expect to understand all of it.

Programming in machine code gives you three main advantages over normal languages: the programs are faster and take up less space, and you also have more control over the innermost corners of the computer. FORTH is already pretty good in all three respects, so there is less need to use machine code on the Ace than on a computer that doesn't use FORTH. However, it can still be useful.

To use machine code, you use a FORTH word **CALL** (address –). **CALL** takes off the stack the address of the start of some machine code, and it starts obeying the machine code instructions there. This carries on until an instruction *jp (iy)* is found. (Each instruction has not only the form coded into bytes, but also a readable name called its *mnemonic. jp (iy)* is a mnemonic form.) The code for *jp (iy)* is two bytes, 253 followed by 233 (you can look up the codes in Appendix A).

The easiest place to put the machine code itself is in the parameter field of a FORTH word, using a defining word

```
DEFINER CODE
DOES>
  CALL
;
```

The action of a word defined by **CODE** is to run the machine code in its parameter field; you set up the parameter field using **C,**.

Here is an example. The machine code instruction *halt* (code 118) makes the processor stop until it receives a signal called an *interrupt*. On the Ace, the rest of the computer gives the processor an interrupt every 50th of a second, so you can use *halt* for timed pauses.

The machine code you need is

```
halt              118
jp (iy)           253, 233
```

so let us put these three bytes into the parameter field of a word **HALT.**

**CODE HALT** 118 **C,** 253 **C,** 233 **C,**

When you execute **HALT**, the action part of **CODE** will **CALL** this machine code. You can now define **PAUSE**.

```
: PAUSE
( length of pause in 50ths of a second —)
0
DO
HALT
LOOP
;
```

If you already know about machine code on the Z80 you'll find it useful to know what some of the restart instructions do.

rst 8 (code 207) outputs a character from the A register. This normally goes to the television screen, but you can make it use a different routine for another device by setting the system variable EXWRCH suitably. (See chapter 24.) This restart uses the A register and the auxiliary B, C, D, E, H and L registers.

rst 16 (code 215) puts the DE register pair onto the FORTH stack. It uses the H and L registers.

Note that the Ace is different from many Z80 based FORTH systems in that it uses the machine stack as the return stack, and sets up the data stack by more laborious means.

147

rst 24 (code 223) takes off the top of the FORTH stack and puts it in the DE register pair. It uses the H and L registers.

rst 32 (code 231) is essentially **ABORT.** The restart instruction should be followed by a byte containing an error code; this is put in the system variable ERR NO before **ABORT** is executed.

Here are a few warnings for those that understand.
1. The IX and IY registers can be used, but they must have their original values restored at the end (but see below regarding IY). All other registers may be freely used, but don't do anything silly with the stack pointer SP.
**2.** Remember that **REDEFINE** and **LOAD** can move words about in the dictionary (see chapter 23, exercise 1). Therefore, if you keep machine code in the dictionary as recommended above with **HALT,** then either it must be relocatable (movable) or you must be very careful with **REDEFINE** and **LOAD.**
The fact that a machine code routine used by **CALL** ends with *jp (iy)* applies to all FORTH words defined as machine code. Such words are called *primitives,* and there are many amongst the 142 FORTH words in ROM. This means that you can affect what happens at the end of each primitive by adjusting the IY register.
Normally, the IY register points to some machine code that checks for errors before carrying on: it checks for space (that the data stack isn't getting too close to the return stack), for stack underflow (on the data stack), and it checks the BREAK key. However, you can save time by making the IY register point straight to the code that goes on to the next word. You don't actually need to know anything about IY registers to do this, because of two words **FAST** and **SLOW.**

**FAST (—)** turns off all the error checking, so that programs run approximately 25% faster.
**SLOW (—)** turns the error checking back on again.

Remember, **FAST** is *dangerous.* You should only use it with words that you have tested thoroughly and know you can trust. Remember especially that the BREAK key won't be tested. **SLOW** isn't much slower, and it's safe.

### Summary
Z80 machine code.
FORTH words: **CALL, FAST, SLOW.**

### Exercises
1. Elaborate on **CODE** so that it gives you more help in setting up the machine code parameter field. For instance, you could leave the machine code bytes on the stack, and tell it how many there are. Maybe it could put in the *jp (iy)* automatically. One common system on FORTH computers is to have a whole **ASSEMBLER** vocabulary that helps you by letting you use mnemonics. For instance, the **ASSEMBLER** vocabulary would have its own word **HALT** defined as

**: HALT**
  118 **C,**
  **;**

(very different from our **HALT**). Then one of the things that **CODE** would do is make **ASSEMBLER** the context vocabulary.

2. Modify **PAUSE** so that it comes out of its pause if you press a key.

3. If you were wondering how the code field of a word worked, I can now tell you. It is the address of some machine code instructions that are obeyed whenever the word is executed. They may make up the entire word — as for a primitive — or they may just explain how to execute a sequence of FORTH compiled words — as in a colon definition.

In a primitive, the code field is just the parameter field address and the parameter field contains the machine code. **DUP** is a primitive, so

### FIND DUP 2+ CALL

and

### FIND DUP @ CALL

both execute **DUP**. There are easier ways, of course.

# Chapter 26

## EXTENDING THE ACE

Extra electronics *(peripherals)* can be plugged in at the back of the Ace by clipping them directly onto the circuit board through a hole in the case. Normally you'd buy such extensions ready-made by someone else and possibly with a tape of programs enabling you to use it. Typical peripherals are extra memory, or connections to printers, and if they are any good they'll be supplied with full instructions.

If you're more adventurous you may feel like making up your own peripherals and you will need to consider how to let your electronics communicate with your FORTH programs, and how physically to connect it to the computer.

First, the communication. The Z80 processor communicates with the rest of the world by using electrical voltages on wires, and the voltages are very crudely measured as being either high or low. These two levels can therefore represent bits (0 or 1). Eight wires grouped together can represent a byte, and there is such a group called the *data bus;* sixteen wires grouped together can represent a single-length integer, and there is such a group called the *address bus.*

The processor uses these to read from or write to memory. When it wants to write a byte to memory, it puts the address on the address bus and the byte on the data bus, and puts out a signal meaning, 'Ahoy there memory! If this is your address then remember the byte on the data bus.' When it wants to read a byte, it puts the address on the address bus and then a signal saying 'If this is your address then please put your remembered byte on the data bus for me.' Then it reads the data bus.

There is a very similar system for what are called *I/O (input/output)* devices such as your peripheral. Again there are 65536 I/O slots (called *ports),* each with its own port address, and the processor communicates with them a byte at a time. When it wants to write a byte to or read a byte from one of them it uses exactly the same system as it did with the memory except that it says 'Ahoy there I/O devices!' and the memory ignores it. It is up to your peripheral to watch out for these signals.

To talk to the I/O ports from a FORTH program, you use two words **IN** and **OUT:** these are the I/O equivalents of the memory words **C@** and **C!**.

> **IN** (address — byte) reads a byte from the port with the given address.
> **OUT** (byte, address —) writes the byte to the port with the given address.

When choosing a port address for your peripheral, avoid ones that are already used by something else. The even addresses are used by the Ace itself, so only use odd addresses.

Here are two simple applications joined together in a single package of electronics. One controls traffic lights, and the other turns a relay on and off. They occupy a single

I/O port (with address 1) and expect the data bytes output by the computer to be coded as follows:

1 turn on red light
2 turn on amber light
3 turn on red and amber lights     } and turn everything
4 turn on green light                   else off
8 turn on relay
0 turn everything off

Here are the FORTH words to use:

```
: CHANGE
  ( data —)
  ( writes to I/O port 1)
  1 OUT
;


: ROFF
  ( —)
  ( turns relay off)
  0 CHANGE
;

: RON
  ( —)
  ( turns relay on)
  8 CHANGE
;

: WAIT
  ( delay — delay)
  DUP 0
  DO
  LOOP
;

DEFINER LIGHT
  ( light code —)
  C,
DOES>
  ( address of light code —)
  C@ CHANGE WAIT
```

**1 LIGHT RED**
**2 LIGHT AMBER**
**3 LIGHT RED&AMB**
**4 LIGHT GREEN**

**: SEQUENCE**
  ( delay — delay)
  **RED RED&AMB GREEN AMBER**
**;**

**: RUNLIGHTS** ✎
  ( delay — delay)
  **BEGIN**
    **SEQUENCE 0**
  **UNTIL**
**;**

e.g. 10000 **RUNLIGHTS** will sequence through the lights repeatedly, using 10000 to determine how long **WAIT** waits at each colour.

This covers the software design; here is a circuit diagram of the electronics needed.

*Traffic Light Controller*                                    Use 2N3904 transistors

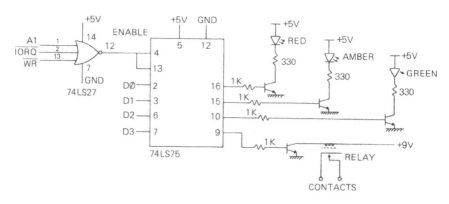

The signals to this circuitry (A1, IORQ and so on) need to be connected to the computer through an *edge connector,* a connector that clips over the back edge of the circuit board. Here is the arrangement of the signals on the computer.

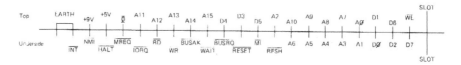

152

Here is another example, this time for input. It reads six switches, each of which can be either open (0) or closed (1), and the byte read in is made of the six corresponding bits with two bits undetermined.

```
DEFINER SWITCH
  ( bit value —)
  C,
DOES>
  ( address of bit value — flag)
  ( leaves 1 if the switch is closed, 0 if open)
  C@ 1 IN AND 0= 0=
;


   1 SWITCH S0
   2 SWITCH S1
   4 SWITCH S2
   8 SWITCH S3
  16 SWITCH S4
  32 SWITCH S5
```

The words **S0**, **...**, **S5** test the corresponding switches and leave a flag on the stack, 1 if the switch is closed.

We could use switch 0 as a Morse key:

```
: MORSE
BEGIN
  S0
    IF
      100 10 BEEP
  THEN
  0
UNTIL
;
```

Here is a word CHECK to check for all the switches being closed, and a word ALARM to raise an alarm unless this happens.

```
: CHECK
  ( — flag)
  1 IN 63 AND 63 =
;
```

```
:  ALARM
      BEGIN
         CHECK 0=
      IF
            100 1000 BEEP
      THEN
         0
      UNTIL
   ;
```

Again we've used I/O port address 1 here. This is the circuit diagram:

*Switch detector*

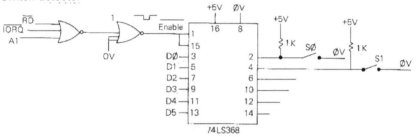

Switches S2 to S5 are similar to S0 and S1, each with a 1K resistor, and are connected to pins 6, 10, 12 and 14.

Our peripherals here used an I/O port, number 1. It is also possible for peripherals to use memory addresses and they are then called *memory-mapped* peripherals. They must be careful not to use memory addresses used by genuine memory (see chapter 24).

All even I/O port addresses are reserved for the Ace's internal use, although it only actually uses eight of them, namely (in hex) FEFE, FDFE, FBEE, F7FE, EFFE, DFFE, BFFE and 7FFE. You can see that the less significant byte is always FE, while if you convert the more significant byte to binary there is one 0 bit and the rest are 1s.

When one of these ports is read from,

(a) Half a row of the keyboard is read – which half row depends on which bit is 0 in the more significant byte of the port address. The least significant five bits of the data show whether a key is pressed (0) or not (1).

(b)  The signal at the EAR socket is read to bit 5 of the data.

(c)  The diaphragm of the loudspeaker is pushed in.

When one of these ports is written to,

(a)  Bit 3 of the data is written to the MIC socket.

(b)  The diaphragm of the loudspeaker is pushed out.

**Summary**

I/O ports, port addresses.

FORTH words: **IN, OUT.**

## Exercises

1. Rewrite the word **CHANGE** so that instead of driving external circuitry it shows something on the television screen.

2. Try this:

```
: NOISE
   [ 16 BASE C! ]
   BEGIN
      FEFE IN FEFE OUT 0
   UNTIL
;
```

Awful, isn't it? Why does the sound change if you press SHIFT? (Remember that the computer is checking for BREAK all the time.)

3. In the traffic lights example, use the relay to control some Christmas tree lights. More ambitiously, if your cassette recorder has a socket through which a microphone can turn it on and off, use the relay to control that.

4. The signals that appear at the back of the circuit board are fairly standard for this sort of Z80-based computer, but they may be in a different arrangement from another type.

For instance, many add-ons for a Sinclair ZX81 will work on the Ace if you wire together the corresponding terminals. The best way would be to make an adaptor with an edge connector to fit the back of the Ace, a piece of printed circuit board to fit in the add-on, and wires in between.

Here is a diagram of the ZX81 signals.

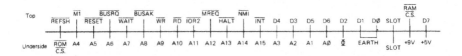

The RAM C.S. and ROM C.S. lines on the ZX81, and the WE on the Ace, don't need connecting.

# Appendix A

## THE CHARACTER SET

Here is the full character set with corresponding Z80 assembler mnemonics.

| Code | Character | hex | Z80 Assembler | —after CB | —after ED |
|------|-----------|-----|---------------|-----------|-----------|
| 0 | new computer line | 00 | nop | rlc b | |
| 1 | | 01 | ld bc,NN | rlc c | |
| 2 | | 02 | ld (bc),a | rlc d | |
| 3 | | 03 | inc be | rlc e | |
| 4 | | 04 | inc b | rlc h | |
| 5 | | 05 | dec b | rlc l | |
| 6 | | 06 | ld b,N | rlc (hl) | |
| 7 | not used | 07 | rlca | rlc a | |
| 8 | | 08 | ex af,af' | rrc b | |
| 9 | | 09 | add hl,bc | rrc c | |
| 10 | | 0A | ld a,(bc) | rrc d | |
| 11 | | 0B | dec be | rrc e | |
| 12 | | 0C | inc c | rrc h | |
| 13 | carriage return | 0D | dec c | rrc l | |
| 14 | not used | 0E | ld c,N | rrc (hl) | |
| 15 | | 0F | rrac | rrca | |
| 16 | | 10 | djnz DIS | rl b | |
| 17 | | 11 | ld de,NN | rl c | |
| 18 | | 12 | ld (de),a | rl d | |
| 19 | | 13 | inc de | rl e | |
| 20 | | 14 | inc d | rl b | |
| 21 | | 15 | dec d | rl l | |
| 22 | | 16 | ld d,N | rl (hl) | |
| 23 | | 17 | rla | rl a | |
| 24 | | 18 | jr DIS | rr b | |
| 25 | | 19 | add hl,de | rr c | |
| 26 | | 1A | ld a,(de) | rr d | |
| 27 | | 1B | dec de | rr e | |
| 28 | not used | 1C | inc e | rr h | |
| 29 | | 1D | dec e | rr l | |
| 30 | | 1E | ld e,N | rr (hl) | |
| 31 | | 1F | rra | rr a | |

| Code | Character | hex | Z80 Assembler | —after CB | —after ED |
|------|-----------|-----|---------------|-----------|-----------|
| 32 | space | 20 | jr nz,DIS | sla b | |
| 33 | ! | 21 | ld hl,NN | sla c | |
| 34 | " | 22 | ld (NN),hl | sla d | |
| 35 | # | 23 | inc hl | sla e | |
| 36 | $ | 24 | inch | sla h | |
| 37 | % | 25 | dec h | sla l | |
| 38 | & | 26 | ld h,N | sla (hl) | |
| 39 | ' | 27 | daa | sla a | |
| 40 | ( | 28 | jr z,DIS | sra b | |
| 41 | ) | 29 | add hl,hl | sra c | |
| 42 | * | 2A | ld hl,(NN) | sra d | |
| 43 | + | 2B | dec hl | sra e | |
| 44 | , | 2C | inc l | sra h | |
| 45 | - | 2D | dec l | sra l | |
| 46 | . | 2E | ld l,N | sra (hl) | |
| 47 | / | 2F | Cpl | sra a | |
| 48 | 0 | 30 | jr nc,DIS | | |
| 49 | 1 | 31 | ld sp,NN | | |
| 50 | 2 | 32 | ld (NN),a | | |
| 51 | 3 | 33 | inc sp | | |
| 52 | 4 | 34 | inc (hl) | | |
| 53 | 5 | 35 | dec (hl) | | |
| 55 | 7 | 37 | scf | | |
| 56 | 8 | 38 | jr c,DIS | srl b | |
| 57 | 9 | 39 | add hl,sp | srl c | |
| 58 | : | 3A | ld a,(NN) | srl d | |
| 59 | ; | 3B | dec sp | srl e | |
| 60 | < | 3C | inc a | srl h | |
| 61 | = | 3D | dec a | srl l | |
| 62 | > | 3E | ld a,N | srl (hl) | |
| 63 | ? | 3F | ccf | srl a | |
| 64 | @ | 40 | ld b,b | bit 0,b | in b,(c) |
| 65 | A | 41 | ld b,c | bit 0,c | out (c),b |
| 66 | B | 42 | ld b,d | bit 0,d | sbc hl,bc |
| 67 | C | 43 | ld b,e | bit 0,e | ld (NN),bc |
| 68 | D | 44 | ld b,h | bit 0,h | ncg |
| 69 | E | 45 | ld b,l | bit 0,l | retn |
| 70 | F | 46 | ld b,(hl) | bit 0,(hl) | im 0 |
| 71 | G | 47 | ld b,a | bit 0,a | ld i,a |
| 72 | H | 48 | ld c,b | bit 1,b | in c,(c) |
| 73 | I | 49 | ld c,c | bit 1,c | out (c),c |
| 74 | J | 4A | ld c,d | bit 1,d | adc hl,bc |
| 75 | K | 4B | ld c,e | bit 1,e | ld bc,(NN) |

| Code | Character | hex | Z80 Assembler | —after CB | —after ED |
|------|-----------|-----|---------------|-----------|-----------|
| 76 | L | 4C | ld c,h | Bit 1,h | |
| 77 | M | 4D | ld c,l | Bit 1,l | reti |
| 78 | N | 4E | ld c,(hl) | Bit 1,(hl) | |
| 79 | O | 4F | ld c,a | Bit 1,a | ld r,a |
| 80 | P | 50 | ld d,b | Bit 2,b | in d,(c) |
| 81 | Q | 51 | ld d,c | Bit 2,c | out (c),d |
| 82 | R | 52 | ld d,d | Bit 2,d | sbc hl,de |
| 83 | S | 53 | ld d,e | Bit 2,e | ld (NN),de |
| 84 | T | 54 | ld d,h | Bit 2,h | |
| 85 | U | 55 | ld d,l | Bit 2,l | |
| 86 | V | 56 | ld d,(hl) | Bit 2,(hl) | im 1 |
| 87 | W | 57 | ld d,a | Bit 2,a | ld a,i |
| 88 | X | 58 | ld e,b | Bit 3,b | in e,(c) |
| 89 | Y | 59 | ld e,c | Bit 3,c | out (c),e |
| 90 | Z | 5A | ld e,d | Bit 3,d | adc hl,de |
| 91 | [ | 5B | ld e,e | Bit 3,e | ld de,(NN) |
| 92 | \ | 5C | ld e,h | Bit 3,h | |
| 93 | ] | 5D | ld e,l | Bit 3,l | |
| 94 | ↑ | 5E | ld e,(hl) | Bit 3,(hl) | im 2 |
| 95 | _ | 5F | ld e,a | Bit 3,a | ld a,r |
| 96 | £ | 60 | ld h,b | Bit 4,b | in h,(c) |
| 97 | a | 61 | ld h,c | Bit 4,c | out (c),h |
| 98 | b | 62 | ld h,d | Bit 4,d | sbc hl,hl |
| 99 | c | 63 | ld h,e | Bit 4,e | ld (NN),hl |
| 100 | d | 64 | ld h,h | bit 4,h | |
| 101 | e | 65 | ld h,l | bit 4,l | |
| 102 | f | 66 | ld h,(hl) | bit 4,(hl) | |
| 103 | g | 67 | ld h,a | bit 4,a | rrd |
| 104 | h | 68 | ld l,b | bit 5,b | in l,(c) |
| 105 | i | 69 | ld l,c | bit 5,c | out (c),l |
| 106 | j | 6A | ld l,d | bit 5,d | adc hl,hl |
| 107 | k | 6B | ld l,e | bit 5,e | ld hl,(NN) |
| 108 | I | 6C | ld l,h | bit 5,h | |
| 109 | m | 6D | ld l,l | bit 5,l | |
| 110 | n | 6E | ld l,(hl) | bit 5,(hl) | |
| 111 | o | 6F | ld l,a | bit 5,a | rld |
| 112 | p | 70 | ld (hl),b | bit 6,b | in f,(c) |
| 113 | q | 71 | ld (hl),c | bit 6,c | |
| 114 | r | 72 | ld (hl),d | bit 6,d | sbc hl,sp |
| 115 | s | 73 | ld (hl),e | bit 6,e | ld (NN),sp |
| 116 | t | 74 | ld (hl),h | bit 6,h | |
| 117 | u | 75 | ld (hl),l | bit 6,l | |
| 118 | v | 76 | Halt | bit 6,(hl) | |
| 119 | w | 77 | ld (hl),a | bit 6,a | |

| Code | Character | hex | Z80 Assembler | —after CB | —after ED |
|------|-----------|-----|---------------|-----------|-----------|
| 120 | x | 78 | ld a,b | bit 7,b | in a,(c) |
| 121 | y | 79 | ld a,c | bit 7,c | out (c),a |
| 122 | z | 7A | ld a,d | bit 7,d | adc hl,sp |
| 123 | { | 7B | ld a,e | bit 7,e | ld sp,(nn) |
| 124 | \| | 7C | ld a,h | bit 7,h | |
| 125 | } | 7D | ld a,l | bit 7,l | |
| 126 | ~ | 7E | ld a,(hl) | bit 7,(hl) | |
| 127 | © | 7F | ld a,a | bit 7,a | |
| 128 | | 80 | add a,b | res 0,b | |
| 129 | | 81 | add a,c | res 0,c | |
| 130 | | 82 | add a,d | res 0,d | |
| 131 | | 83 | add a,e | res 0,e | |
| 132 | | 84 | add a,h | res 0,h | |
| 133 | | 85 | add a,l | res 0,l | |
| 134 | | 86 | add a,(hl) | res 0,(hl) | |
| 135 | | 87 | add a,a | res 0,a | |
| 136 | not used | 88 | adc a,b | res 1,b | |
| 137 | | 89 | adc a,c | res 1,c | |
| 138 | | 8A | adc a,d | res 1,d | |
| 139 | | 8B | adc a,e | res 1,e | |
| 140 | | 8C | adc a,h | res 1,h | |
| 141 | | 8D | adc a,l | res 1,l | |
| 142 | | BE | adc a,(hl) | res 1,(hl) | |
| 143 | | 8F | adc a,a | res 1,a | |
| 144 | | 90 | sub b | res 2,b | |
| 145 | | 91 | sub c | res 2,c | |
| 146 | | 92 | sub d | res 2,d | |
| 147 | | 93 | sub e | res 2,e | |
| 148 | | 94 | sub h | res 2,h | |
| 149 | | 95 | sub l | res 2,l | |
| 150 | | 96 | sub (hl) | res 2,(hl) | |
| 151 | | 97 | sub a | res 2,a | |
| 152 | | 98 | sbc a,b | res 3,b | |
| 153 | | 99 | sbe a,c | res 3,c | |
| 154 | | 9A | sbc a,d | res 3,d | |
| 155 | | 9B | sbc a,e | res 3,e | |
| 156 | not used | 9C | sbc a,h | res 3,h | |
| 157 | | 9D | sbc a,l | res 3,l | |
| 158 | | 9E | sbc a,(hl) | res 3,(hl) | |
| 159 | | 9F | sbc a,a | res 3,a | |
| 160 | □ | A0 | and b | res 4,b | ldi |
| 161 | inverse ! | A1 | and c | res 4,c | cpi |
| 162 | inverse " | A2 | and d | res 4,d | ini |
| 163 | inverse # | A3 | and e | res 4,e | outi |

| Code | Character | hex | Z80 Assembler | —after CB | —after ED |
|------|-----------|-----|---------------|-----------|-----------|
| 164 | inverse $ | A4 | and h | res 4,h | |
| 165 | inverse % | A5 | and l | res 4,l | |
| 166 | inverse & | A6 | and (hl) | res 4,(hl) | |
| 167 | inverse ' | A7 | and a | res 4,a | |
| 168 | inverse ( | A8 | xor b | res 5,b | ldd |
| 169 | inverse ) | A9 | xor c | res 5,c | cpd |
| 170 | inverse * | AA | xor d | res 5,d | ind |
| 171 | inverse + | AB | xor e | res 5,e | outd |
| 172 | inverse , | AC | xor h | res 5,h | |
| 173 | inverse – | AD | xor l | res 5,l | |
| 174 | inverse . | AE | xor (hl) | res 5,(hl) | |
| 175 | inverse / | AF | xor a | res 5,a | |
| 176 | inverse 0 | B0 | or b | res 6,b | ldir |
| 177 | inverse 1 | B1 | or c | res 6,c | cpir |
| 178 | inverse 2 | B2 | or d | res 6,d | inir |
| 179 | inverse 3 | B3 | or e | res 6,e | otir |
| 180 | inverse 4 | B4 | or h | res 6,h | |
| 181 | inverse 5 | B5 | or l | res 6,l | |
| 182 | inverse 6 | B6 | or (hl) | res 6,(hl) | |
| 183 | inverse 7 | B7 | or a | res 6,a | |
| 184 | inverse 8 | B8 | cp b | res 7,b | lddr |
| 185 | inverse 9 | B9 | cp c | res 7,c | cpdr |
| 186 | inverse : | BA | cp d | res 7,d | indr |
| 187 | inverse ; | BB | cp e | res 7,e | otdr |
| 188 | inverse < | BC | cp h | res 7,h | |
| 189 | inverse = | BD | cp l | res 7,l | |
| 190 | inverse > | BE | cp (hl) | res 7,(hl) | |
| 191 | inverse ? | BF | cp a | res 7,a | |
| 192 | inverse @ | C0 | ret nz | set 0,b | |
| 193 | inverse A | C1 | pop bc | set 0,c | |
| 194 | inverse B | C2 | jp nz,NN | set 0,d | |
| 195 | inverse C | C3 | jp NN | set 0,e | |
| 196 | inverse D | C4 | call nz,NN | set 0,h | |
| 197 | inverse E | C5 | push bc | set 0,l | |
| 198 | inverse F | C6 | add a,N | set 0,(hl) | |
| 199 | inverse G | C7 | rst 0 | set 0,a | |
| 200 | inverse H | C8 | ret z | set 1,b | |
| 201 | inverse I | C9 | ret | set 1,c | |
| 202 | inverse J | CA | jp z,NN | set 1,d | |
| 203 | inverse K | CB | | set 1,e | |
| 204 | inverse L | CC | call z,NN | set 1,h | |
| 205 | inverse M | CD | call NN | set 1,l | |
| 206 | inverse N | CE | adc a,N | set 1,(hl) | |
| 207 | inverse O | CF | rst 8 | set 1,a | |

| Code | Character | hex | Z80 Assembler | —after CB | —after ED |
|------|-----------|-----|---------------|-----------|-----------|
| 208 | inverse P | D0 | ret nc | set 2,b | |
| 209 | inverse Q | D1 | pop de | set 2,c | |
| 210 | inverse R | D2 | jp nc,NN | set 2,d | |
| 212 | inverse T | D4 | call nc,NN | set 2,h | |
| 213 | inverse U | D5 | push de | set 2,l | |
| 214 | inverse V | D6 | sub N | set 2,(hl) | |
| 215 | inverse W | D7 | rst 16 | set 2,a | |
| 216 | inverse X | D8 | ret c | set 3,b | |
| 217 | inverse Y | D9 | exx | set 3,c | |
| 218 | inverse Z | DA | jp c,NN | set 3,d | |
| 219 | inverse [ | DB | in a,(N) | set 3,e | |
| 220 | inverse \ | DC | call c,NN | set 3,h | |
| 221 | inverse [ | DD | prefixes instructions using ix | set 3,l | |
| 222 | Inverse ↑ | DE | sbc a,N | set 3,(hl) | |
| 223 | inverse _ | DF | rst 24 | set 3,a | |
| 224 | inverse £ | E0 | ret po | set 4,b | |
| 225 | inverse a | E1 | pop hl | set 4,c | |
| 226 | inverse b | E2 | jp po,NN | set 4,d | |
| 227 | inverse c | E3 | ex (sp),hl | set 4,e | |
| 228 | inverse d | E4 | call po,NN | set 4,h | |
| 229 | inverse e | E5 | push hl | set 4,l | |
| 230 | inverse f | E6 | and N | set 4,(hl) | |
| 231 | inverse g | E7 | rst 32 | set 4,a | |
| 232 | inverse h | E8 | ret pe | set 5,b | |
| 233 | inverse i | E9 | jp (hl) | set 5,c | |
| 234 | inverse j | EA | jp pe,NN | set 5,d | |
| 231 | inverse g | E7 | rst 32 | set 4,a | |
| 235 | inverse k | EB | ex de,hl | set 5,e | |
| 236 | inverse l | EC | call pe,NN | set 5,h | |
| 237 | inverse m | ED | | set 5,l | |
| 238 | inverse n | EE | xor N | set 5,(hl) | |
| 239 | inverse o | EF | rst 40 | set 5,a | |
| 240 | inverse p | F0 | ret p | set 6,b | |
| 241 | inverse q | F1 | pop af | set 6,c | |
| 242 | inverse r | F2 | jp p,NN | set 6,d | |
| 243 | inverse s | F3 | di | set 6,e | |
| 244 | inverse t | F4 | call p,NN | set 6,h | |
| 245 | inverse u | F5 | push af | set 6,l | |
| 246 | inverse v | F6 | or N | set 6,(hl) | |
| 247 | inverse w | F7 | rst 48 | set 6,a | |
| 248 | inverse x | F8 | ret m | set 7,b | |
| 249 | inverse y | F9 | ld sp,hl | set 7,c | |
| 250 | inverse z | FA | jp m,NN | set 7,d | |

| Code | Character | hex | Z80 Assembler | —after CB | —after ED |
|------|-----------|-----|---------------|-----------|-----------|
| 251 | inverse { | FB | ei | set 7,e | |
| 252 | inverse \| | FC | call m,NN | set 7,h | |
| 253 | inverse } | FD | prefixes instructions using iy | set 7,l | |
| 254 | inverse ~ | FE | cp N | set 7,(hl) | |
| 255 | inverse © | FF | rst 56 | set 7,a | |

# Appendix B

## ERRORS

There are two sorts of errors. The more harmless sort occurs when the computer finds an unrecognized word in the input buffer: it turns the cursor to ▓ and gives you a chance to correct it. Note that ▓ doesn't invariably show an error; there are other circumstances - for instance when you use **EDIT** - when it just means that the computer is giving you a chance to alter the input buffer.

Other errors are more serious and cause ERROR to be shown on the screen, with an error code. They clear the data stack, the return stack and the input buffer, and any incomplete definition at the end of the dictionary is taken off.

Here are the various error codes, with their meanings and possible causes.

*Code Meaning*

1   Not enough memory. Either you tried to put too many items on the data stack or the return stack, or you tried to put a new entry in the dictionary for which there was not enough room. See Chapter 5.

2   Data stack underflow. The stack has apparently less than no items on it. See Chapter 5, Exercise 4.

3   BREAK pressed. BREAK is normally shifted space; during tape operations and **BEEP** it is just space.

4   You have tried to use a compiling word in interpret mode, i.e. outside a word definition. Can be caused by **IF, ELSE, THEN, BEGIN, UNTIL, WHILE, REPEAT, DO, LOOP, +LOOP, ;, DOES>, RUNS>, (, ."** or a compiling word defined by **COMPILER.**

5   A word is not properly structured. **IF ... THEN, IF ... ELSE ... THEN, BEGIN ... UNTIL, BEGIN ... WHILE ... REPEAT, DO ... LOOP, DO ... +LOOP, : ... ;, DEFINER ... DOES> ... ;** and **COMPILER ... RUNS> ... ;** must all match up and nest properly. See Chapter 10.

6   The name of a new word is either too short (no name at all) or too long (64 characters or more). Can be caused by :, **DEFINER, COMPILER, CREATE, CONSTANT, VARIABLE** or any defining word of your own made using **DEFINER.**

7   **PICK** or **ROLL** used with operand 0 or negative. Note — an operand of - 32768

won't cause error 7. See Chapter 6, Exercise 2.

8  Overflow in floating point arithmetic: the result of a calculation is too big for the Ace's range of floating point numbers. Can be caused by **F+**, **F−**, **F\*** or **F/**. A common cause is trying to divide by zero.

9  Trying to print in input buffer. Can be caused by **AT** or **PLOT**.

10  Tape error.
   (a)  In **SAVE** or **BSAVE** – either no file name supplied, nothing to save.
   (b)  In **VERIFY** or **BVERIFY** - the verification has failed
   (c)  In **LOAD** – the file is too long to fit in the remaining memory.
   (d)  In **BLOAD** or **BVERIFY** – : the file is too long to fit in: the length specified.
   (e)  In **LOAD**, **VERIFY**, **BLOAD** or **BVERIFY** there was some kind of reading fault. Either the volume setting is wrong or possibly the file is corrupted.

11  Error In **REDEFINE** or **FORGET**
   In **REDEFINE**, either the newest word in the current vocabulary is not the newest word of all, or the old words not found or is in ROM, or the old word was defined by **DEFINER** or **COMPILER** but the new word wasn't, or there is not enough space left in memory (there needs to be enough space to hold two copies of the new word after the old one has been, deleted).
   In **FORGET**, the context and current vocabularies are different.

12  Incomplete definition in dictionary - certain operation;; are not then allowed. Can be caused by **REDEFINE,** any tape operation, or any defining word (as listed under Error 6). This error rectifies itself by taking the incomplete definition out of the dictionary. You probably started a definition (with :, and then **DEFINER** or **COMPILER**), returned to execute mode with **[**, and then attempted the illegal operation.

13  Word not found, or is ROM or is **FORTH**. Can be , caused by **FORGET**, **LIST** or **EDIT**.

14  Word unlistable ; caused by **LIST** or **EDIT**. Only words defined by :, **DEFINER** or **COMPILER** are listable.

# Appendix C

## THE JUPITER ACE - FOR REFERENCE

### Characters and Keyboard

The Ace uses an ASCII character set with the following special provisions:

| code | meaning |
|------|---------|
| 0 | Separates logical lines in the input buffer |
| 13 | Carriage return |
| 16-23 | Mosaic characters |
| 16 | ▪ |
| 17 | ◪ |
| 18 | ◪ |
| 19 | ▬ |
| 20 | ▐ |
| 21 | ▌ |
| 22 | ▞ |
| 23 | ◣ |
| 96 | £ |
| 127 | © |
| 128--255 | Inverse video versions of characters 0 to 127. |

The shapes of all characters 0 to 127 are stored in RAM and can be redefined by the user. Each shape is an 8 x 8 array of dots. and is stored as 8 consecutive bytes in RAM, with the top row of dots at hex address 2C00 + 8 * ASCII code and the bottom row at hex address 2000 + 8 * ASCII code + 8. in each row, the leftmost dot is the most significant bit (1 = white).

All characters, including upper and lower case can be entered from the keyboard. SHIFT is used for capitals and control functions (shifted digits), SYMBOL SHIFT for symbols − punctuation etc. Three special typing modes are turned on and off (independently of each other) by corresponding shifted digit keys: CAPS LOCK converts lower case letters to capitals, INVERSE VIDEO converts all characters to inverse video, and GRAPHICS converts characters to those with codes 0 to 31 or 128 to 159, by resetting bits 5 and 6 of the ASCII code All keys repeat if held down.

The input buffer occupies the bottom of the T-V screen and can expand upwards to accommodate extra typing. All typing is inserted immediately to the left of the cursor, which may change its form to reflect different typing modes (normally ▪, C for CAPS LOCK on, G for GRAPHICS; also ? when the computer offers a chance to retype the buffer). The cursor can be moved about with shifted 5, 6, 7 and 8, DELETE deletes the character just to the left of the cursor, and DELETE LINE deletes the entire input buffer (but see **EDIT).**

When ENTER is pressed, the FORTH interpreter takes words out of the input buffer, copies them up to the top part of the screen, and executes them (but see **INVIS).** It continues until either the buffer is empty or an undefined word is found.

Shifted SPACE usually acts as BREAK, giving ERROR 3.


## FORTH Vocabulary

In the descriptions of the words,

| | |
|---|---|
| n | means a single length integer |
| d | means a double length integer |
| u | means unsigned |
| f | means a floating point number |
| I | indicates that a word is immediate |
| C | indicates that a word can only he used in compile mode. |

| | | |
|---|---|---|
| ! | | (n, address —) |
| | | Stores the single length integer n at the given address in memory. |
| # | | (ud1 — ud2) |
| | | Used in formatted output. Generates one digit from the unsigned double length integer ud1 and holds it in the pad. The unsigned double length integer ud2 is the quotient when ud1 is divided by the number base (at **BASE).** |
| #> | | (ud — address, n) |
| | | Finishes formatted output, leaving the address and length (n) of the resultant string. |
| #S | | (ud — 0,0) |
| | | Applies # repeatedly (at least once) until the double length number left on the stack is 0. |
| CI | | ( Starts a comment, terminated by ). |
| * | | (n1, n2 — n1 * n2) |
| */ | | (n1, n2, n3 — (n1 * n2)/n3) |
| | | The intermediate product n1 * n2 is held to double length. |
| */MOD | | (n1, n2, n3 — remainder, quotient of (n1 * n2)/n3) |
| | | As in */, n1 * n2 is held to double length. |
| + | | (n1, n2 — n1 +n2) |
| CI +LOOP | | (n —) |
| | | Used with **DO**. Adds n to the loop counter, and loops back if the loop counter is now less than the limit (if n > 0) or greater than the limit (if n < 0). |
| , | | (n —) |
| | | Encloses the single length integer n in the dictionary. |
| _ | | (n1, n2 — n1 — n2) |
| . | | (n —) |
| | | Prints n to the television screen, followed by a space. |

166

| | | |
|---|---|---|
| CI | ." | (—) |
| | | Prints the following string, terminated by ". |
| | / | (n1, n2 — n1/n2) |
| | | Single length signed integer division. |
| | /MOD | (n1, n2 — remainder, quotient of n1/n2) |
| | | The remainder has the same sign as the dividend n1 |
| | 0< | (n — flag) |
| | | flag is 1 if n is negative. |
| | 0= | (n — flag) |
| | | flag is 1 if n = 0. |
| | 0> | (n — flag) |
| | | flag is 1 if n is positive. |
| | 1+ | (n — n+1) |
| | 1- | (n — n—1) |
| | 2+ | (n — n+2) |
| | 2- | (n — n—2) |
| | : | Introduces colon definitions. |
| CI | ; | Terminates colon, **DEFINER** and **COMPILER** definitions. |
| | < | (n1, n2 — flag) |
| | | flag is 1 if n1 < n2. |
| | <# | (—) |
| | | Initiates formatted output. |
| | = | (n1, n2 — flag) |
| | | flag is 1 if n1 = n2. |
| | > | (n1, n2 — flag) |
| | | flag is 1 if n1 > n2. |
| | >R | (n —) |
| | | Transfers top of data stack to return stack; it can be copied back using I. |
| | ?DUP | (n — n,n) if n ≠ 0, |
| | | (n—n)   if n=0. |
| | @ | (address — n) |
| | | Leaves on stack the single length integer at the given address. |
| | **ABORT** | Clears the data and return stacks, deletes any incomplete definition left in the dictionary, prints 'ERROR' and the byte from address 3C3D (hex) if the byte is non-negative, empties input buffer, and returns control to the keyboard. |
| | **ABS** | (n — absolute value of n) |
| | **ALLOT** | (n —) |
| | | Encloses n bytes in the dictionary, without initializing them. |
| | **AND** | (n1, n2 — n1 AND n2) |
| | | Bitwise Boolean operation. |
| | **ASCII** | Takes the next word from the input buffer, and yields the ASCII code of its first character. If compiling, then compiles this as a literal. |

e.g.　　**: STARS 0 DO ASCII * EMIT LOOP ;**
　　　　　(—ASCII code)　　(if interpreting)
　　　　　(—)　　　　　　　(if compiling)

**AT**　　　(line, column —)
Sets print position to line and column numbers on the stack. There are 23 lines (0 to 22) and 32 columns (0 to 31). The column number is taken modulo 32, and ERROR 9 if trying to print in the input buffer at the bottom.

**BASE**　　(— 15423)
A 1-byte variable containing the system number base.

**BEEP**　　(m, n —)
Plays a note on the loudspeaker. 8*m = period in micro-seconds, n = time in milliseconds.

CI **BEGIN**　　(—)
Used with either **UNTIL** or **WHILE . . . REPEAT.**

**BLOAD**　　name　　(m, n —)
Load at most n bytes of bytes type cassette file 'name' starting at address m. ERROR 10 if the file has more than n bytes.

**BSAVE**　　name(m, n —)
Save n bytes to bytes type cassette file 'name' starting at address m.

**BVERIFY**　　name (m, n —)
Verify at most n bytes from bytes type cassette file 'name' against RAM starting at address m. ERROR 10 if the file has more than n bytes. For **BLOAD** and **BVERIFY,** if m = 0, then starts at the address the bytes were saved from. If n = 0, then doesn't care about length.

**C!**　　(n, address —)
Stores the less significant byte of n at the given address.

**C,**　　(n —)
Encloses the less significant byte of n in the dictionary.

**C@**　　(address — byte)
Fetches the contents of the given address.

**CALL**　　(address —)
Executes Z80 machine code at address on stack. The code is terminated by *jp (iy).*
e.g. in hex
**DEFINER CODE DOES> CALL ;**
**CODE** EI FB **C,** FD **C,** E9 **C,**
The word **EI** will enable interrupts.

**CLS**　　(—)
Clears the screen and sets the print position to top left of screen.

CI **COMPILER**　　Used with **RUNS>** for defining new compiling words, i.e.

words that are used within word definitions to give an immediate effect of compiling some information into the dictionary. (This is traditionally done with **IMMEDIATE**, but **COMPILER** ... **RUNS>** works better with **EDIT** etc.)

The new compiling word compiles a 2-byte address pointing to a run-time action, and an optional operand field.

The format is

n **COMPILER** name
    compiling routine
  **RUNS>**
    action routine
;

n is expected on the stack, and is the number of bytes in the optional operand field. If it is -1, then the first two bytes of the operand field are expected (by **EDIT** etc) to contain the total length of the rest of the operand field.

'name' is the name of the new compiling word.

'compiling routine' is a piece of FORTH that will set up the operand field — it is up to you to ensure that the number of bytes set up equals the value of n from the stack.

'action routine' is a piece of FORTH to perform the run-time action. It is entered with the address of the operand field on the stack.

Note – **LIST** and **EDIT** will not list the operand fields, nor will **REDEFINE** adjust them.

**CONSTANT** name (n —)
Defines a constant with the given name and value n.

**CONTEXT** (— 15411)
A system variable pointing to the context vocabulary.

**CONVERT** (ud1, addr1 — ud2, addr2)
Accumulates digits from text into an unsigned double length number ud1 : for each digit. the double length accumulator is multiplied by the system number base and the digit (converted from ASCII) is added on. The text starts at addr1 + 1. addr2 is the address of the first unconvertable character, ud2 is the final value of the accumulator.

**CR** (—)
Outputs a carriage return character to the television.

**CREATE** name (—)
Defines a new word with a header and empty parameter field. When executed, the new word stacks its parameter field address.

**CURRENT** (– 15409)
A system variable pointing to the current vocabulary.

**D+** (d1, d2 — d1 +d2)

|   |   |   |
|---|---|---|
| | | double length integer addition. |
| | **D<** | (d1, d2 — flag) |
| | | flag is 1 if of the signed double length integers, d1 < d2. |
| | **DECIMAL** | (—) |
| | | sets system number base to ten. |
| | **DEFINER** | Used with **DOES>** to define new defining words, i.e. words that themselves define new words. |

The format is

**DEFINER** name
    defining routine
**DOES>**
    action routine
;

'name' is the name of the new defining word; when executed it will set up the header of a new word and use its defining routine to set up the parameter field. When this new word in its turn is executed, its parameter field will be put on the stack and the action routine will be executed.

|   |   |   |
|---|---|---|
| | **DEFINITIONS** | (—) |
| | | The context vocabulary is made to be current vocabulary as well. |
| | **DNEGATE** | (d - -d) |
| | | Double length integer negation. |
| CI | **DO** | (limit, initial value —) |
| | | Sets up a **DO** loop, initializing the loop counter to the initial value. The limit and loop counter are stored on the return stack. See **LOOP** and **+LOOP**. |
| CI | **DOES>** | See **DEFINER**. |
| | **DROP** | (n —) |
| | | Throws away the top of the stack. |
| | **DUP** | (n — n, n) |
| | | Duplicates the top of the stack. |
| | **EDIT** name | (—) |
| | | Lists word 'name' at bottom of screen to be edited. Lists 18 lines at a time, then waits for editing until ENTER is pressed. A new version of the word is entered at the end of the dictionary. |
| | | While editing, cursor up and cursor down are needed to move the cursor from one line to another. DELETE LINE deletes one line. |
| CI | **ELSE** | (—) |
| | | Used with **IF** and **THEN**. |
| | **EMIT** | (character —) |
| | | Writes the character to the television screen. |
| | **EXECUTE** | (compilation address —) |

|  |  |
|---|---|
|  | Executes the word with the given compilation address. |
| **EXIT** | **(—)** |
|  | Exits immediately from the word in whose definition it is contained. Cannot be used between **DO** and **LOOP** or **+LOOP,** nor between **>R** and **R>**. |
| **F*** | (f1, f2 — f1*f2) |
|  | Multiplies top two floating point numbers and leaves result on the stack. |
| **F+** | (f1, f2 — f1+f2) |
|  | Adds top two floating point numbers. |
| **F-** | (f1, f2 — f1—f2) |
|  | Subtracts top two floating point numbers. |
| **F.** | (f — ) |
|  | Prints floating point number. |
|  | If 1.0E-4 ≤ f < 1.0E9, then f is printed without an exponent and with a decimal point in the appropriate place. If f is outside this range, then it is printed in standard form f'En where 0 ≤ f' < 10 and -64 ≤ n ≤ 62. |
|  | Input may be either form, but only 6 significant figures are accepted — further digits are ignored. |
|  | Floating point numbers are stored as 3 bytes of binary coded decimal mantissa and 1 byte for sign and decimal exponents. |
| **F/** | (f1, f2 — f1/f2) |
|  | Divides two floating point numbers. |
| **FAST** | Fast mode — runs without error checks. See **SLOW**. |
| **FIND** | (— compilation address) |
|  | Leaves compilation address of first word in input buffer, if defined in context vocabulary; else 0. |
| **FNEGATE** | (f - -f) |
|  | Floating point negation. |
| **FORGET** name | (—) |
|  | Erases the word 'name' and all subsequently defined words from the dictionary. |
| **FORTH** | (—) |
|  | Makes the standard vocabulary **FORTH** the context vocabulary. |
| **HERE** | (— address) |
|  | Leaves the address of one byte past the end of the dictionary. |
| **HOLD** | (character —) |
|  | Used in formatted output to hold the character in the pad. |
| **I** | (— loop counter) |
|  | Copies the top of the return stack to the data stack. This will be either the loop counter for the innermost **DO** ... **LOOP**, or the number most recently transferred by **>R**. |
| **I'** | ( - limit) |

Copies second number down on return stack to data stack (so in a **DO** loop, it copies the limit of the loop).

CI **IF** (n —)

Used in the form

**IF ... THEN**

or

**IF ... ELSE ... THEN**

In the first form, if n is non-zero then the words between **IF** and **THEN** are executed; otherwise they are skipped over.

In the second form, if n is non-zero then the words between **IF** and **ELSE** are executed and those between **ELSE** and **THEN** are skipped over, while if n is zero then the words between **IF** and **ELSE** are skipped over and those between **ELSE** and **THEN** are executed.

**IMMEDIATE** (—)

The most recent word in the current vocabulary is made *immediate, so* that it will execute even in compile mode.

**IN** (port address — data byte)

Inputs a data byte from an I/O port.

**INKEY** (— ASCII code)

Reads the keyboard. Puts ASCII value on the stack if a key is pressed, 0 otherwise.

**INT** (f — n)

Converts signed floating point number to signed single length integer. Truncates towards zero.

**INVIS** Suppresses copy-up mechanism and OK. See **VIS**.

**J** (— loop counter)

Copies the third entry on the return stack to the data stack. This will be either the loop counter for the second innermost **DO** loop, or the number put on the return stack by the third most recent **>R**.

**LEAVE** (—)

Forces termination of a **DO** loop at the next **LOOP** or **+LOOP** by setting the loop counter equal to the limit.

**LINE** Interprets input buffer as a normal FORTH line.

**LIST** name (—)

Lists word 'name' on screen. It must have been defined by :, **DEFINER,** or **COMPILER.** Lists about 18 lines at time and waits for a key depression (shifted space breaks).

CI **LITERAL** (n —)

Compiles the top of the stack into a word definition as a literal.

**LOAD** name (—)

Searches for a dictionary cassette file 'name' and loads it in, adding it to end of old dictionary. Writes to the screen all files found on tape. For best results, turn the tone control on the tape recorder right down (as bass as possible) and the volume control to about three quarters maximum. See **SAVE.**

Cl **LOOP**  ( — )

Like **+LOOP,** but the number added on to the loop counter is **1.**

**MAX**  (n1, n2 – max (n1, n2))

Calculates the larger of two numbers.

**MIN**  (n1, n2 — min (n1, n2))

Calculates the smaller of two numbers.

**MOD**  (n1, n2 — remainder n1/n2)

The remainder has the same sign as the dividend n1

**NEGATE**  (n - -n)

**NUMBER**  Takes a number from the start of the input buffer. Leaves the number and a non-zero address on the stack. (The address is the compilation address of a literal compiler, so that if you then say **EXECUTE,** the literal compiler compiles the number into the dictionary as a literal — for an integer it is 4102. for a floating point number 4181.)

If no valid number, then leaves just 0 on the stack.

**OR**  (n1, n2 — n1 OR n2)

Bitwise Boolean operation.

**OUT**  (data byte, port address —)

Outputs a data byte to an I/O port.

**OVER**  (n1, n2 – n1, n2, n1)

**PAD**  (– 9985)

Stacks the address of the 254-byte work pad.

**PICK**  (n1 – n2)

Copies the n1-th stack entry (after dropping n1 itself) to the top. Error 7 if n1 ≤ 0.

**PLOT**  (x, y, n –)

Plots pixel (x, y) with plot mode n.

  n = 0  unplot

       1  plot

       2  move

       3  change

If n > 3, takes value modulo 4.

**QUERY**  Clears input buffer, then accepts characters until ENTER pressed. Buffer can be edited as usual and is limited to 22 lines.

**QUIT**  (—)

Clears return stack, empties input buffer and returns control to the keyboard.

**R>**  (– entry from return stack)

Transfers top entry on return stack to data stack.

**REDEFINE** name  (–)

Takes word 'name' and replaces it with the most recent word

in the dictionary. Updates entire dictionary to take changes into account.

Most commonly used as

**EDIT** name

**REDEFINE** name

CI **REPEAT** (—)

Used in construction **BEGIN** . . . **WHILE** . . . **REPEAT**. Causes a jump back to just after **BEGIN**.

**RETYPE** Allows user to edit input line. Turns cursor to ▊. (c.f. **QUERY** which first clears input buffer.)

**ROLL** (n —)

Extracts the nth stack value to the top of the stack, after dropping n itself, and moves the remaining values down to fill the vacated position. Error 7 if n ≤ 0.

**ROT** (n1, n2, n3 — n2, n3, n1)

CI **RUNS>** See **COMPILER**.

**SAVE** name (—)

Saves the entire dictionary in RAM on a dictionary type cassette file with the given name. Makes a noise on the internal loudspeaker. See **VERIFY** and **LOAD,** and also **BSAVE, BVERIFY** and **BLOAD.**

**SIGN** (n —)

In formatted output, holds a minus sign in the pad if n is negative.

**SLOW** (—)

Slow mode with error checking. See **FAST.**

**SPACE** (—)

**EMITs** a space.

**SPACES** (n —)

**EMITs** n spaces, if n ≥ 1.

**SWAP** (n1, n2 — n2, n1)

CI **THEN** Used with **IF.**

**TYPE** (address, n —)

**EMITs** n characters from memory starting at the address.

**U\*** (un1, un2 — double length (un1 \* un2))

Multiplies two unsigned single length integers together to give an unsigned double length product.

**U.** (un —)

Prints the unsigned single length integer un to the television screen, followed by a space.

**U/MOD** (ud1, un2 — un3, un4)

In unsigned arithmetic throughout, divides the double length integer ud1 by the single length integer un2 to give a single length remainder un3 and a single length quotient un4.

**U<** (un1, un2 — flag)

|  |  |  |
|---|---|---|
| | | The flag is 1 if of the two unsigned single length integers un1 is less than un2. |
| | **UFLOAT** | (un — f) |
| | | Converts unsigned, single length integer to floating point. |
| CI | **UNTIL** | (n —) |
| | | Used in **BEGIN** . . . **UNTIL**. Loops back to **BEGIN** if n = 0. |
| | **VARIABLE** name | |
| | | (n —) |
| | | Sets up a variable with the given name, and initializes its value to n. |
| | **VERIFY** name | (—) |
| | | Verifies dictionary on tape against dictionary in RAM. See **SAVE**. |
| | **VIS** | Allows copy-up mechanism and OK. See **INVIS**. |
| | **VLIST** | List dictionary to screen, including words in ROM. (No pause after 18 lines.) |
| | **VOCABULARY** name | |
| | | (—) |
| | | Defines a new vocabulary with the given name. |
| CI | **WHILE** | (n —) |
| | | Used in **BEGIN** . . . **WHILE** . . . **REPEAT**. If n = 0 then skips over to just past **REPEAT**. |
| | **WORD** text | (delimiter — address) |
| | | Takes text out of the input buffer up as far as a delimiter, and copies it to pad, starting at the second byte there. Puts the length (not including delimiter) in the first byte of the pad, and stacks the address of the first byte of the pad. |
| | | At most 253 characters are taken from the input buffer. If there are more left before the delimiter, then the first byte of the pad shows 254. Initial delimiters are ignored. |
| | **XOR** | (n1, n2 — n1 XOR n2) |
| | | Bitwise Boolean XOR (exclusive or). |
| I | **[** | (—) |
| | | Enters interpret mode. |
| | **]** | (—) |
| | | Enters compile mode. |

# Appendix D

## QUICK GUIDE FOR 'FORTH' ENTHUSIASTS

Ace FORTH is based on FORTH-79, the principle differences being:

1. The Ace does not use screens at all. Input and output uses a cassette recorder, and stores either a dictionary in its compiled form (lists of compilation addresses) or raw bytes from memory. See **SAVE, VERIFY, LOAD, BSAVE, BVERIFY, BLOAD.**

2. The Ace can decompile words as a matter of course — see **LIST** and **EDIT**. It can also change already compiled words in the dictionary and adjust all the compilation addresses and pointers - see **REDEFINE** and **LOAD**.

3. There are some facilities for floating point arithmetic — **F+, F—, F\*. F/, F., FNEGATE, INT, UFLOAT.**

4. **DEFINER** . . **DOES>** replaces **:** . **CREATE** . . . **DOES>** for defining new defining words; there is a corresponding pair **COMPILER** . . . **RUNS>** for defining new compiling words.

5.    There are extra words **ASCII, AT, BEEP, CALL, CLS, FAST, IN, INKEY, INVIS, LINE NUMBER, OUT, PLOT, RETYPE, SLOW, VIS.**

6. Ace FORTH lacks **', +!, -TRAILING, 79-STANDARD, >IN, ?, CMOVE, COMPILE, COUNT, DEPTH, EXPECT, FILL, KEY, MOVE, NOT, STATE, [COMPILE]**.

# Index

**The Author**

After studying mathematics for eight years, first at King's College, Cambridge and then at Leeds University where he gained a PhD in algebra, Steven Vickers turned to computer programming and played a large part in developing the Sinclair ZX81 and ZX Spectrum.

In 1980 he read *The Hitchhiker's Guide to the Galaxy* and, realising that its high content of factual errors made it unreliable for practical use, decided to rewrite it. The result was what is by now probably the best-selling computer manual ever, for the ZX81. He also wrote the manual for the ZX Spectrum.

In 1982 he and Richard Altwasser set up Jupiter Cantab Ltd and designed the Jupiter Ace.

The computer language FORTH is becoming widely available on microcomputers, for which many remarkable features make it ideal. With FORTH you can easily write faster, more effective programs.
This book, a course in FORTH programming written for the Jupiter Ace and provided free with it, can also be used on its own to explain clearly and readably how to use this intriguing language.

Originally printed by
**The Leagrave Press Ltd**
Luton & London

This 35th Anniversary Edition
published by
**Andrews UK Limited**
Luton, UK

www.ingramcontent.com/pod-product-compliance
Lightning Source LLC
Chambersburg PA
CBHW051052050326
40690CB00006B/694